W9-ARS-334

Ladders to Success on the State Exam

READING, HIGH SCHOOL

Ladders to Success on the State Exam, Reading, High School
280NA
ISBN-10: 1-60471-119-1
ISBN-13: 978-1-60471-119-6

Written by: Emily Adler, Mary Harvey, Shaun McCormack, and Peter Victor
Cover Image: Cover illustration by Mark Collins/Deborah Wolfe Ltd.

Triumph Learning® 136 Madison Avenue, 7th Floor, New York, NY 10016
Kevin McAliley, President and Chief Executive Officer

© 2009 Triumph Learning, LLC

All rights reserved. No part of this publication may be reproduced in whole or in part, stored in a retrieval system, or transmitted in any form or by any means, electronic, mechanical, photocopying, recording or otherwise, without written permission from the publisher.

Printed in the United States of America.

10 9 8 7 6 5 4 3

Ladders to Success on the State Exam

Table of Contents

Diagnostic Test

excerpt from

Dracula (1897)

by Bram Stoker

4 May—I found that my landlord had got a letter from the Count, directing him to secure the best place on the coach for me; but on making inquiries as to details he seemed somewhat reticent, and pretended that he could not understand my German.

This could not be true, because up to then he had understood it perfectly; at least, he answered my questions exactly as if he did.

He and his wife, the old lady who had received me, looked at each other in a frightened sort of way. He mumbled out that the money had been sent in a letter, and that was all he knew. When I asked him if he knew Count Dracula, both he and his wife crossed themselves and simply refused to speak further.

Just before I was leaving, the old lady came up to my room and said in a hysterical way: "Must you go? Oh! Young Herr, must you go?" She was in such an excited state that she seemed to have lost her grip of what German she knew, and mixed it all up with some other language which I did not know at all. I was just able to follow her by asking many questions. When I told her that I must go at once, and that I was engaged on important business, she asked again:

"Do you know what day it is?" I answered that it was the fourth of May. She shook her head as she said again:

"Oh, yes! I know that! But do you know that it is the eve of St. George's Day? Do you not know that tonight, when the clock strikes midnight, all the evil things in the world will have full sway? Do you know where you are going, and what you are going to?" She was in such evident distress that I tried to comfort her, but without effect. Finally, she went down on her knees and implored me not to go; at least to wait a day or two before starting.

It was all very ridiculous but I did not feel comfortable. However, there was business to be done, and I could allow nothing to interfere with it.

1. What detail from the passage indicates that the old woman is concerned about the main character's well being?

    A. I told her that I must go at once.

    B. Both he and his wife crossed themselves and simply refused to speak further.

    C. There was business to be done.

    D. The old lady came up to my room and said in a hysterical way: "Must you go?"

2. Which of the following lines from the passage is an opinion?

    A. He and his wife...looked at each other in a frightened sort of way.

    B. But do you know that it is the eve of St. George's Day?

    C. It was all very ridiculous but I did not feel comfortable.

    D. I was just able to follow her by asking many questions.

3. Based on the passage, what can you predict may happen next?

    A. The main character will decide not to go to the castle.

    B. The older couple will board up the house for the winter.

    C. The main character will proceed to the castle.

    D. The carriage will break a wheel on the way to the castle.

4. If you wanted to find an overview of transportation in the late 1800s, where would you look?

    A. an encyclopedia

    B. an atlas

    C. a dictionary

    D. a periodical

5. Which of the statements below correctly contrasts the main character with the old woman?

    A. He is more hygienic than the old woman.

    B. The old woman is more fearful and superstitious than the young man.

    C. Unlike the main character, the old woman is married.

    D. The old woman cannot read.

6. What happens first in the passage?

    A. The landlord receives a letter from the count.

    B. The couple tries and fails to learn German.

    C. The visitor secures a coach and leaves to see the count.

    D. The group observes St. George's Day.

7. What is the main idea of the passage?

   A. In order to travel through countryside, one must take a carriage.

   B. A man is on his way to visit with a sinister Count.

   C. An older couple is superstitious but hospitable.

   D. All evil things come out on the eve of St. George's Day.

8. In the passage, why do the husband and wife seem to forget their German and sometimes refuse to answer their visitor's questions?

   A. They are afraid someone is listening.

   B. They have taken a vow of silence.

   C. They are too spooked to answer the visitor.

   D. They do not speak German at all.

9. Based on context clues, what is the meaning of the word *reticent* in the first paragraph?

   A. thoughtful

   B. provocative

   C. outspoken

   D. quiet

10. What is the author's purpose in the passage?

   A. to summarize

   B. to persuade

   C. to justify

   D. to entertain

excerpt from

Against the Spanish Armada (1588)

Queen Elizabeth I's speech

My loving people, we have been persuaded by some who are careful and concerned for our safety, to take heed how we commit ourselves to war, for fear of treachery. But I assure you, I do not desire to live to distrust my faithful and loving people. Let tyrants rule by fear. I have always believed my chief strength and safeguard is in the loyal hearts and good will of my subjects. And therefore I come to you at this time, in the midst and heat of the battle, not for my recreation or sport, but being resolved to live or die amongst you all. I will lay down, for my God, and for my kingdom, and for my people, my honor and my blood, even the dust.

I know I have but the body of a weak and feeble woman, but I have the heart of a king, and of a king of England, too. I think foul scorn that Parma or Spain, or any prince of Europe, should dare to invade the borders of my realms. Rather than any dishonor should grow by me or while I wear the crown, I myself will take up arms. I myself will be your general, judge, and rewarder of every one of your virtues in the field. I know already, by your forwardness, that you have deserved rewards and crowns. We do assure you, on the word of a prince, they shall be duly paid you. In the meantime, my lieutenant general shall be in my stead. No previous prince ever commanded a more noble and worthy subject. Without the slightest doubt of your obedience to my general, of your concord in the camp, and of your valor in the field, we shall shortly have a famous victory over the enemies *of my God, of my kingdom, and of my people.*

11. Why are certain words in the last sentence of the passage italicized?

  A. because these words should be emphasized

  B. because another person is speaking

  C. because these words should be looked up in the dictionary

  D. because these are the most recognizable words in the speech

12. Which of the following is the BEST summary of the passage?

  A. I am a female ruler and therefore must go to battle to prove that I am patriotic.

  B. I will give ample rewards to those who are valiant in battle.

  C. Spain is ruled by tyrants, but England is ruled by me, your benevolent queen.

  D. Despite being a woman, I will take up arms against our oppressors alongside my countrymen.

13. Which of the following is one of Queen Elizabeth I's opinions?

  A. She believes Spain is foolish to defend itself against England.

  B. She believes that the loyalty of her people is her greatest asset.

  C. She believes female rulers are stronger and wiser than male rulers.

  D. She believes that she has a weak and feeble body, but the heart of a king.

14. What happened first in the passage?

  A. The British air force invaded Spain.

  B. The queen repeated herself.

  C. People warned beware of treachery.

  D. Queen Elizabeth I decided to go into battle herself.

15. Based on the passage, what is a reasonable generalization that a reader might make about life during the 16th century?

  A. Much emphasis was placed on courtship and romance at the expense of intellectual pursuits.

  B. Many Europeans worked together to create a sense of unity among their citizens.

  C. Countries were very nationalistic and sometimes warred with each other in order to increase their power and wealth.

  D. Most people in England were very progressive in their views toward women.

16. Based on context clues in the passage, who is the "subject" Queen Elizabeth I refers to when she says, "No previous prince ever commanded a more noble and worthy subject"?

  A. the citizens whom she is addressing

  B. her lieutenant general

  C. the war with Spain

  D. London, England

17. What is Queen Elizabeth I's purpose in the passage?

    A. to trick the Spanish army into capitulating

    B. to introduce herself to the public for the first time

    C. to entertain her citizens with a fairy tale

    D. to persuade her citizens that together they will win the war

18. Which of the following sentences from the passage shows a contrast?

    A. I will lay down, for my God, and for my kingdom, and for my people, my honor and my blood, even the dust.

    B. I know I have but the body of a weak and feeble woman, but I have the heart of a king, and of a king of England, too.

    C. Rather than any dishonor should grow by me or while I wear the crown, I myself will take up arms.

    D. I myself will be your general, judge, and rewarder of every one of your virtues in the field.

19. In the queen's speech, you can infer that she is responding to which of her citizens' doubts?

    A. doubt about her courage and valor because of her gender

    B. doubt about her sword fighting ability

    C. doubt about her loyalty to England

    D. doubt about her intelligence because of her gender

20. Which of the following is NOT a cause for Queen Elizabeth I to fight?

    A. The Spaniards have invaded.

    B. The queen wishes to show solidarity with her soldiers.

    C. Her lieutenant general has challenged her to take up arms.

    D. She does not want to be mistaken for a weak ruler.

The Love Song of J. Alfred Prufrock (1917)

by T.S. Eliot

Let us go then, you and I,
When the evening is spread out against the sky,
Like a patient etherized upon a table;
Let us go, through certain half-deserted streets,
The muttering retreats,
Of restless nights in one-night cheap hotels
And sawdust restaurants with oyster shells:
Streets that follow like a tedious argument
Of insidious intent
To lead you to an overwhelming question...
Oh, do not ask, "What is it?"
Let us go and make our visit.

In the room the women come and go,
Talking of Michelangelo. . .

And indeed there will be time
For the yellow smoke that slides along the street,
Rubbing its back upon the windowpanes;
There will be time, there will be time
To prepare a face to meet the faces that you meet;
There will be time to murder and create,
And time for all the works and days of hands
That lift and drop a question on your plate;
Time for you and time for me,
And time yet for a hundred indecisions,
And for a hundred visions and revisions,
Before the taking of a toast and tea...

In the room the women come and go,
Talking of Michelangelo. . .

And indeed there will be time
To wonder, "Do I dare?" and, "Do I dare?"
Time to turn back and descend the stair,
With a bald spot in the middle of my hair—
(They will say: "How his hair is growing thin!")
My morning coat, my collar mounting firmly to the chin,
My necktie rich and modest, but asserted by a simple pin,
(They will say: "But how his arms and legs are thin!")
Do I dare
Disturb the universe?
In a minute there is time
For decisions and revisions that a minute will reverse.

For I have known them already, known them all—
Have known the evenings, mornings, afternoons,
I have measured out my life with coffee spoons,
I know the voices dying with a dying fall,
Beneath the music from a farther room.
So how should I presume?

21. What is the author's purpose in the poem?

A. to refute

B. to summarize

C. to entertain

D. to persuade

22. Which of these lines from the poem includes a metaphor?

A. Let us go, through certain half-deserted streets

B. There will be time to murder and create

C. In the room the women come and go

D. I have measured out my life with coffee spoons

23. Read the following lines from the poem.

When the evening is spread out against the sky,
Like a patient etherized upon a table;

Based on the context clues, what is the MOST LIKELY meaning of *etherized*?

A. upright

B. sedated

C. clothed

D. awake

24. Based on the passage, you can infer that the last two stanzas use questions

A. to show the speaker is confused and indecisive.

B. to show the speaker is curious and playful.

C. to show the speaker is forgetful.

D. because the audience already knows the answers.

25. Which resource would you use to find the meaning of the word *insidious*?

A. thesaurus

B. dictionary

C. almanac

D. encyclopedia

26. What is one possible heading for the fifth stanza?

A. When I Am Old

B. When I Go to My First Ball

C. How to Dress for Company

D. Cosmology Lessons

27. Which line from the poem is an example of a simile?

    A. Time to turn back and descend the stair

    B. The yellow smoke that rubs its muzzle

    C. And time yet for a hundred indecisions,

    D. Streets that follow like a tedious argument

28. Based on the poem, you can conclude that the speaker

    A. is wary of youth.

    B. often thinks about time.

    C. has many friends.

    D. is overconfident.

29. Which line from the passage describes the effect of the line "With a bald spot in the middle of my hair"?

    A. (They will say: "But how his arms and legs are thin!")

    B. (They will say: "How his hair is growing thin!")

    C. Let us go and make our visit

    D. I know the voices dying with a dying fall

30. Which of the following is the BEST paraphrase of the first stanza?

    A. We should go on this walk without unnecessary delay.

    B. We have an appointment. Let's be sure to get there on time.

    C. The city streets are quiet but exciting.

    D. There are many restaurants and hotels in town.

Protecting Our World

In the environmentalism debate, there have always been opponents. Protecting our natural world seems to come at the expense of fostering human development and productivity. If we restrict access to oil, then oil is in greater demand and its price goes up. Suddenly, a person's daily expenses rise. Their heat costs more. Driving their car costs more. Even turning on the stove to boil water is more expensive. People spend a lot of money on taxes every year. It's terrible to ask the average person to not go to work because the cost of getting there is too high.

In recent years though, people have begun to discover that perhaps environmentalism and human development are part of the same interconnected web. No longer opponents, but rather systems that must work together. After all, humans are part of the natural world, too. Yes, gas prices will go up if we restrict access to oil. But the air we breathe will also be increasingly polluted if we use gas at our current rate. We think that we are using our resources for our betterment, but lately we learn that we may in fact be doing ourselves and our planet a great deal of harm.

The concept of sustainability emerged as an alternative vision of environmentalism. Some people call it a paradigm shift—a change in the way we look at our world. Since environmental, economic, social and physical well-being are interconnected, sustainability advocates are considering these impacts holistically rather than piece-meal.

Our population is surging, especially in the poorest countries. This makes our access to resources more limited. In order to continue to support those on Earth, we need to conserve what we have and change our behavior in smart, useful ways. It is no longer enough to make sure to separate paper and plastic in the recycling bins. Sustainability asks the recycler to look at all those plastic water bottles they have accumulated. Instead of continuing to buy, consume, and recycle bottled water, the individual could save even more waste, energy, and even cash by using filtered water from the tap instead.

According to the United Nations Decade of Education for Sustainable Development, "Sustainability is about 'thinking about forever'…committing ourselves to the common good by thinking differently, considering things previously forgotten, broadening our perspectives, clarifying what we value, connecting with our neighbors, and providing hope for future generations." Sustainability is about considering our environmental impact in the fullest sense, rather than with blinders on. Then we may truly be able to affect both our natural world and our lifestyle with intelligence, commitment and, most of all, success.

31. Which of the following is the BEST alternate title for the passage?

    A. The Raging Earth

    B. Human Versus Planet

    C. Our Sustainable World

    D. On Sustaining Economic Growth

32. In the last paragraph, the phrase "with blinders on" is an example of

    A. a simile.

    B. hyperbole.

    C. onomatopoeia.

    D. an idiom.

33. The statement, "It's terrible to ask the average person to not go to work because the cost of getting there is too high" is an opinion because

    A. some people might not think it is so terrible.

    B. the statement has been proven false.

    C. it has been confirmed by economic research.

    D. an almanac does not include this information.

34. The sentence "Driving their cars cost more" is an example of

    A. a main idea.

    B. a detail.

    C. an inference.

    D. a generalization.

35. In the chain of events that lead to higher oil costs, what happens first?

    A. Due to population growth, more gas is consumed.

    B. People begin to drive cars with better gas mileage.

    C. Implementing sustainability leads to more oil use.

    D. The government issues rebates to reduce energy costs.

36. According to the passage, how does environmentalism compare to sustainability?

    A. Both are about eating organic meat.

    B. Both are concerned with available housing development.

    C. Both are concerned with the environment.

    D. Both are about the United Nations making policy decisions.

37. Based on the passage, what is a reasonable inference you can make about the author?

    A. The author always recycles because it is good for the environment.

    B. The author believes that environmentalism is better than sustainability.

    C. The author believes people are more important than ecosystems.

    D. The author believes sustainability is a very important concept.

38. Which generalization is MOST reasonable, based on the passage?

    A. As populations grow, people compete for more of Earth's resources.

    B. Since most of Earth is water, there is no need to conserve this resource.

    C. We should start recycling all of our waste, not just plastics.

    D. Environmentalists do not understand that people need money.

39. What is the BEST paraphrase of the sentences below?

If we restrict access to oil, then oil is in greater demand and its price goes up. Suddenly, a person's daily expenses rise. Their heat costs more. Driving their car costs more. Even turning on the stove to boil water is more expensive.

    A. Heat is expensive, but not as expensive as gasoline.

    B. The more oil we have available, the more expensive it becomes.

    C. People have a lot of daily needs that cost money.

    D. When oil is expensive, it affects many aspects of daily life.

40. Read the definitions of *resource* below.

resource, (re-sors) *noun* **1.** a natural feature or phenomenon that enhances the quality of life **2.** compatible wealth **3.** a source of information or expertise **4.** a means of spending one's leisure time

Which definition of resource is used in the sentence, "This makes our access to resources more limited"?

    A. definition 1

    B. definition 2

    C. definition 3

    D. definition 4

excerpt from

The Sorrow Songs (1903)

by W.E.B. Du Bois

The true African folk song still lives in the hearts of those who have heard them truly sung and in the hearts of the African people. What are these songs, and what do they mean? I know little of music and can say nothing in technical phrase, but I know something of men, and knowing them, I know that these songs are the articulate message of the slave to the world. They seem to tell us in their eagerness that life was joyous to the black slave, careless and happy. I can easily believe this of some, of many. But not all the past South, though it has risen from the dead, can see only the heart-touching witness of these songs. In truth, it is the music of an unhappy people, of the children of disappointment. It tells of death and suffering, of unvoiced longing toward a truer world, of misty wanderings and hidden ways.

The songs are indeed the siftings of centuries. The music is far more ancient than the words, and in it we can trace signs of how it has been passed down. My grandfather's grandmother was seized by an evil Dutch trader two centuries ago. Coming to the valleys of the Hudson and Housatonic, she was black, little, and lithe. She looked longingly at the hills and shivered and shrank like a wilting flower. Often she crooned a wordless melody of indecipherable sounds to the child between her knees, thus:

Do ba - na co - ba, ge - ne me, ge - ne me!
Do ba - na co - ba, ge - ne me, ge - ne me!
Ben d' nu - li, nu - li, nu - li, nu - li, ben d' le.

The child sang it to his children and they to their children's children. So over two hundred years, it has travelled down to us. We sing it to our children, knowing as little as our fathers what its words may mean, but knowing well the meaning of its music.

This was African music. It may be seen now in larger form in the strange chant which heralds "The Coming of John":

"You may bury me in the East,
You may bury me in the West,
But I'll hear the trumpet sound in that morning,"
It is the voice of exile.

41. What is the main idea in this passage?

    A. African folk songs tell stories and have been passed down for generations.

    B. Slave life was extremely difficult.

    C. "The Coming of John" is one of the most important folk songs.

    D. The original African folk songs were difficult to understand.

42. The phrase "shrank like a wilting flower" is an example of

    A. a metaphor.

    B. a simile.

    C. personification.

    D. hyperbole.

43. Based on context clues, what is the meaning of *indecipherable* in the second paragraph?

    A. easy to understand

    B. difficult to understand

    C. too quiet to be heard

    D. melodic

44. What is W.E.B. Du Bois's purpose in this passage?

    A. to entertain

    B. to exemplify

    C. to persuade

    D. to inform

45. Which of the following is a contrast between old African folk songs and the songs from Du Bois's time?

    A. The older songs tended to be more heartfelt.

    B. The new songs were happier than the old songs.

    C. The new songs turned the old songs' sounds into words.

    D. The new songs were sung only by non-Africans.

46. Which of the following is the MOST LIKELY cause for the woman to have looked "longingly at the hills and shivered and shrank like a wilting flower"?

    A. She does not like walking long distances, especially uphill.

    B. Her child is too heavy to carry.

    C. She wishes she could sing in English.

    D. She misses her old home and feels daunted by her hard life.

47. Where would you be MOST LIKELY to find the passage?

    A. on a Web site

    B. in a dictionary

    C. in an almanac

    D. in an encyclopedia

48. Which of the following statements is a good paraphrase of the first paragraph?

   A. The speaker is not much of a musician so it is sometimes difficult to hear the power of African folk songs.

   B. African folk songs are alive and well in people's memories.

   C. African folk songs tell evocative stories of hope and suffering. They are the slave's communication of his/her plight.

   D. The speaker disagrees with those who think African folk songs are happy. They are really quite regretful.

49. What is a reasonable generalization you can make about W.E.B. Du Bois's perspective?

   A. He believes in working hard and reaping the rewards of your labor.

   B. He believes songs were the way slaves kept their heritage alive over years of persecution and exile.

   C. He believes African folk songs are difficult to understand because they are so technically complicated.

   D. He believes in tending to one's children first and foremost.

50. In the sentence below, what word or phrase is a clue that the statement is an opinion?

   They seem to tell us in their eagerness that life was joyous to the black slave, careless and happy.

   A. seem to tell

   B. their eagerness

   C. life was

   D. careless and happy

Boating in January

Most people think that January weather is too cold to go boating on the lake, but Arthur and his father don't agree. In the winter, the lake is an endless sapphire, and there is a wonderful calm and quiet peace. Theirs is often the only boat on the lake, and they sometimes feel they are the only two souls for miles and miles around. They also catch more fish than they do during the summer months.

One January morning, Arthur and his father bundled in warm gloves, scarves, and hats, and set out for a day of fishing. The weather forecast had promised a clear day, so Arthur was surprised to see a sky like a bruise. Heavy storm clouds clustered toward the south and east. "Don't worry," Arthur's father said. "The snow will mean we'll catch a lot of fish. And if it gets too cold or stormy, we'll bring the boat back home."

By noon, however, neither Arthur nor his father had felt a single nibble. The fish were sleepyheads at the bottom of the lake. Furthermore, the cold had become a thick wall, reddening their faces and weakening their arms as they cast their fishing poles. Arthur tried not to complain, but when icy snowflakes began pelting them like pebbles, he pleaded with his father to turn the boat around.

"Maybe I should have gone home when we first saw those clouds," said Arthur's father.

Arthur agreed. "I guess we learned our lesson."

The storm churned above them, and the once-blue lake was now as black as mud. With agonizing effort, Arthur's father managed to turn the boat around and head for home. Arthur helped out as much as possible, his muscles straining, his heart a nervous kettle-drum in his chest.

Nowadays, Arthur and his father still insist that boating on the lake is a lot of fun, even during the middle of winter. But now they're very cautious about when they choose to go fishing. They listen to the weather forecast, and remain as cautious as cats. Certain days can be nightmares, they know, if the weather doesn't cooperate.

51. What is the author's purpose for writing this passage?

    A. to inform

    B. to entertain

    C. to persuade

    D. to describe

52. What is the main idea of the passage?

    A. Arthur and his father get lost while canoeing on a lake.

    B. People should go boating on a lake during the winter.

    C. Arthur and his father enjoy boating in January because they catch a lot of fish.

    D. The storm churned above them, and the once-blue lake was now as black as mud.

53. Read the sentence from the passage.

Heavy storm clouds clustered toward the south and east.

What does *clustered* mean?

    A. gathered in a group

    B. gathered sparingly

    C. gathered one at a time

    D. gathered and then disappeared

54. In the first paragraph, "the lake is an endless sapphire" means

    A. the lake is large and bright blue.

    B. the lake is a valuable gemstone.

    C. the lake is hard and frozen.

    D. the lake is dangerous and likely to have violent storms.

55. When did snowflakes pelt Arthur and his father?

    A. before they listened to the weather report

    B. before the storm clouds clustered

    C. after they turned the boat around

    D. after the storm clouds clustered

56. How does fishing in January differ from fishing in the summer?

    A. Arthur and his father catch more fish in January than during the summer.

    B. Arthur and his father catch less fish in January than during the summer.

    C. Arthur and his father are the only ones on the lake during the summer.

    D. Arthur and his father rent a boat in January, but fish from a dock in the summer.

57. What made the lake turn as black as mud?

    A. The fish started swimming to the surface.

    B. The storm churned, darkening the sky and thereby the lake.

    C. Arthur and his father left the fishing poles in the water too long.

    D. Arthur and his fathered rowed rigorously, churning up mud.

58. Which of the following answers is an opinion?

   A. One January morning, Arthur and his father bundled in warm gloves, scarves, and hats, and set out for a day of fishing.

   B. With agonizing effort, Arthur's father managed to turn the boat around and head for home.

   C. "Maybe I should have gone home when we first saw those clouds," said Arthur's father.

   D. By noon, neither Arthur nor his father had felt a single nibble.

59. If Arthur and his father hear a blizzard warning during the weather forecast, they will MOST LIKELY

   A. not go boating on the lake.

   B. bring umbrellas with them.

   C. ignore the forecast.

   D. bring hot cocoa with them.

60. Use the chart to answer the question.

Monday	Tuesday	Wednesday	Thursday	Friday
Snow High: 27° Low: 12°	Some snow showers High: 30° Low: 20°	Mostly sunny High: 35° Low: 23°	Mostly sunny High: 38° Low: 25°	Increasing Clouds High: 30° Low: 22°

Arthur and his father would like to go fishing on the nicest and warmest day. Which day would be BEST for them to go fishing?

   A. Monday

   B. Tuesday

   C. Thursday

   D. Friday

University of the Plains

Application for Undergraduate Admission

(Before filling out this application, please make sure to visit our Web site, www.plainsuniversity.com, for detailed instructions, and an overview of the campus.)

Personal Data

Laley	*Barney*	*2/22/90*	
Family Name	Given Name	Birth Date	Social Security Number

Home Address

Rosebud St	*Madison*	*WI*	*13010*
Number and Street	City	State	Zip Code

Please check if you would like to be considered for early decision admission. ☐

Declared or anticipated major, or check undecided: _____ undecided: ☐

For a list of majors, please view a PDF of the school catalog at www.plainsuniversity.edu/PDF.

Supplemental Documents

Please include with your application:
• a personal essay stating why you wish to attend University of the Plains
• two letters of recommendation from teachers of character witnesses
• an official sealed high school transcript
• an official SAT test report

Please write a concise summary *(from most recent to least recent)* of your extracurricular activites in the space below.

_____

_____

_____

_____

Please tell us something unique about yourself that we might otherwise be unable to discern from your application.

_____

_____

_____

61. What information is missing from the student's home address?

   A. social security number

   B. street number

   C. street name

   D. zip code

62. Barney has played the following two sports and worked at the following two jobs during high school.

   1. Camp counselor 2003–2007

   2. Grocery clerk 2008

   3. Soccer 2004–2008

   4. Bowling 2005–2006

   The application says to list extracurricular activities from most recent to least recent. Which activity should Barney list LAST?

   A. 1

   B. 2

   C. 3

   D. 4

63. Which of the following statements would NOT be appropriate in the section that asks for unique personal information?

   A. I am an avid political junkie who cannot get enough of election debates and coverage.

   B. As a child, I loved eating chocolate and eventually created an amateur chocolatier shop in my parents' kitchen.

   C. Although I wanted to slither off the field when my saxophone broke during a marching band competition, I continued to march with perseverance.

   D. I am extremely attractive, with a 5'8" thin frame, startling blue eyes, and long, straight brown hair.

64. What reference material can you use to find out what a social security number is?

   A. the periodical *Science Times*

   B. a search engine Web site

   C. *The World Almanac Book of Facts*

   D. the newest edition of a thesaurus

65. What word goes in the blank below?

   The letters of recommendations will explain _____ the student.

   A. the letter writer's opinion of

   B. how the letter writer first heard about

   C. the SAT scores and GPA of

   D. why University of the Plains was chosen by

66. What is the BEST heading for the section of the application that includes a summary of Barney's extracurricular activities and unique personal information?

   A. Extra Thoughts

   B. Inquiries and Curiosities

   C. Additional Information

   D. Extracurricular Activities

67. Barney wants to study engineering. Where would it be MOST appropriate to include this information?

   A. on the line above social security number

   B. in the section on previous extracurricular activities

   C. on the write-on line for anticipated major

   D. He should not include this information on the form.

68. Barney has begun filling out his application. According to the instructions, he already should have

   A. visited the school's campus.

   B. retrieved a black pen to use.

   C. considered his job options.

   D. viewed the school's Web site.

69. If Barney will be submitting the application today, what can you infer?

   A. He has taken the SAT test.

   B. He has finished writing his recommendation.

   C. He has filled out other forms before.

   D. He will be submitting the application online.

70. In his personal essay, Barney writes, "My family has lived all across the country. At each new home, my passion has been to search out the craziest site within 50 miles. In Marfa, Texas, I went to see the 'Mystery Lights,' which look like three giant orbs glowing in the distance. In Tennessee, I visited the former home of E.T. Wickham who built statues of Paul Bunyon, his Blue Ox, and John F. Kennedy on his property. My mom said Wickham must have been a weirdo. I told her, 'Mom, the term is eccentric.'"

This is an example of

   A. compare and contrast.

   B. a summary.

   C. a text feature.

   D. a generalization.

Lesson 1 • Author's Purpose

An **author's purpose** is a reason for writing. Authors write to inform, to entertain, or to persuade. The chart below shows some examples of the most common author's purposes.

Purpose	Example
To inform	George Washington was born on February 22, 1732, in Westmoreland County, Virginia.
To entertain	The sun set way out beyond the mountains and sea, casting pinkish, purple swirls across the horizon and within the clouds.
To persuade	Run—don't walk—to your nearest car dealership as this is the sales event of the year.

Example

Before you begin this lesson, take this quiz to show what you know about author's purpose. Read this newspaper classified advertisement. Then answer the questions.

1956 Fender Stratocaster Guitar

Up for sale, a 1956 Fender Stratocaster in 100% original, collector-grade condition. Guitar looks great and plays perfectly. It's a feathery 8 pounds and has tone for days!

The original electronics are in perfect working condition. All plastic is intact. The original two-tone sunburst finish shows some significant wear—totally understandable for a guitar of its age.

Don't miss out on this once-in-a-lifetime chance to own a smart investment and true American icon! $50,000 firm.

Circle the letter of the best answer.

1. What is author's purpose?

   A. to describe the guitar

   B. to persuade someone to buy the guitar

   C. to persuade someone to play the guitar

   D. to entertain with a story about the guitar

2. Which is the MOST persuasive phrase in the last paragraph?

   A. "Don't miss out."

   B. "smart investment"

   C. "once-in-a-lifetime chance"

   D. "$50,000 firm."

DIRECTIONS
Read this passage about baseball. Use the Reading Guide to help you recognize the author's purpose. Then answer the questions on the next page.

A Serious Game

I must have been thirteen or so, back in 6th grade at an all-day baseball tournament. Mark charged the mound at least five times that day. He would start it off anytime the ball came within a foot of him. He'd scream out, "Bench clearing brawl!" Then he'd charge the mound and tackle the pitcher. Then the rest of the kids on his team would pile on top of them. Then our team would pile on top of his team. Everyone would laugh so hard they could barely catch their breath. The poor pitcher would be crushed at the bottom. Usually you had to wait your turn to pitch in our ball games. Not today. Nobody wanted to pitch because it'd only be a matter of time before you found yourself at the bottom of a twenty-kid pileup.

Wow, could Mark hit! Charging the mound was just for kicks. Mark took the game pretty seriously. He was easily the best hitter in our town. He never played in the official town league, though, because his parents would never pay for him to join. So he just used our all-day tournaments to show everyone he was the best. We all knew it. He could hit the ball harder and farther than anyone else.

Mark could also catch anything hit anywhere near him. He could climb the fence and make outs out of would-be homers that would've just barely cleared the fence. What a bummer that was. He did it to me dozens of times over the years. It wasn't fair because when Mark hit a homerun, it was gone for good—over the fence and on top of the pavilion on the other side of the street. He was the best.

Reading Guide

What is the author's purpose in writing this passage?

....

How has the author tried to entertain the reader?

....

Are there any persuasive elements in this last paragraph?

Circle the letter of the best answer.

1. What is the author's main purpose in the passage?

   A. to teach readers about baseball

   B. to prove to readers that Mark was the best player

   C. to entertain readers with a story from his youth

   D. to convince readers that bench clearing brawls are dangerous

2. Which sentence from the passage is MOST clearly meant to entertain readers?

   A. "He was the best."

   B. "He'd scream out, 'Bench clearing brawl!'"

   C. "Wow could Mark hit!"

   D. "He never played in the official town league, though, because his parents would never pay for him to join."

3. Which sentence in the third paragraph is the MOST persuasive?

   A. "He was the best."

   B. "He could also catch anything hit anywhere near him."

   C. "He could climb the fence and make outs out of would-be homers that would've just barely cleared the fence."

   D. "It wasn't fair."

4. Which sentence is the MOST informative?

   A. "He could also catch anything hit anywhere near him."

   B. "He could hit the ball harder and farther than anyone else."

   C. "He could climb the fence and make outs out of would-be homers that would've just barely cleared the fence."

   D. "He was the best."

Authors usually try to entertain readers with fiction, and inform or persuade readers with nonfiction. **Persuasive writing** is sometimes filled with bias, or an author's personal opinion about a topic. **Propaganda** is biased, persuasive, and often dishonest writing. Scare tactics are sometimes used to persuade people to believe propaganda. At other times, authors write poetry or prose with the simple intention of expressing their ideas and feelings, or to describe something in detail.

Example

Read the following campaign speech. Look for examples of propaganda.

Vote for Change

Our community is at a crossroad. We are faced with a dwindling tax base and falling property values. Our schools are overcrowded. Our police and fire departments are understaffed and overworked. Mayor Boom's regime has left our town in disarray. It's vital that we end this administration's rule of tyranny and bring power back to the people. The alternatives are dire: a collapse of our local economy; a community brought to its knees by gang violence because of a weakened police force; the worst high school graduation rate in the state. This is why I am running for office.

As mayor, I promise to turn the tide and return our town to the glory we used to know and expect. There will be no more pointing fingers or ignoring the problems facing our community. I will tackle our issues head-on, taking every citizen's needs and desires into account. My administration will be "the people's administration." All voices will be represented.

My first goal will be to reduce tax burdens on the poor. By increasing taxes on the wealthiest ten percent of our community, we will ease the burden on the impoverished and raise funds for our schools, our police force, and our fire department. Lower tax rates will draw new residents to buy homes in our town. This will help return property values to where they used to be and further reduce the tax burden on current residents. But none of this will happen if I don't get your vote. The choice is yours: continue under the negligent tyranny of Mayor Doug Boom, or make a vote for the future with me, Sterling Plunder.

Fill in the boxes below with the author's purpose in each of the three paragraphs of the campaign speech. Note any possible use of bias or propaganda.

Paragraph 1	
Paragraph 2	
Paragraph 3	

DIRECTIONS
Read this passage about digital music and audio players. Use what you have learned about author's purpose to answer the questions. Make a graphic organizer on a separate sheet of paper to organize your thoughts.

MP3s and Digital Audio Players

Digital audio players have changed the way people listen to music. Up until the late 1990s, it was pretty difficult for a person to carry their entire music library around with them. It was especially cumbersome for people with large collections.

The first digital audio player was released in 1997 to support the growing popularity of MP3s, which are relatively small digital music files. When the MP3 file format first came out, people listened to them on their computers. MP3 players gave music fans a way to take all of their digital music on the road with them.

A peer-to-peer file sharing network on the Internet kicked MP3 trading into overdrive. The service peaked in February 2001 when over 25 million unique users logged on to download free MP3s. The Web site was loved by music fans and hated by most of the recording industry. Lesser-known artists could reach a large audience by offering their music for free on the site. But established artists saw music that they had spent time and money to make being passed around for free. The recording industry sued the site and the service was eventually taken offline. The site was the best peer-to-peer network ever.

The popularity of the file-sharing Web site and free MP3s opened the floodgates for a new brand of digital audio player, which is now the most popular digital audio player out there. Other companies have tried and failed to compete with this new technology.

1. What is the author's purpose in writing this article?

   HINT: The author includes a lot of information.

   _____

2. Which sentence from the third paragraph is the MOST persuasive?

   HINT: One sentence states an opinion.

   _____

   _____

3. What is the author's purpose in the last paragraph?

   HINT: Look for information, facts, and opinions.

   _____

DIRECTIONS
Read this editorial. Then answer the questions.

Save Snaky River

For many centuries, the cool water of the Snaky River has run clear and clean, but all it took was a few months—less than a year—for the people in our town to ruin it. Here are some reasons why you should care.

Littering in our river harms the plants and animals that live in and near it. An ecosystem of living things is a delicate balance. Take away the clean water that the ecosystem needs to thrive and that balance of life is thrown out of kilter. The flora and fauna become unhealthy and may die.

If plants and animals do not matter to you, maybe children do. I often see children playing near the river, and sometimes swimming in it. Not only is the water now filthy, but some of the debris has sharp edges that could injure a child's feet or legs.

Dirty, polluted water offers an open invitation for mosquitoes, mice, rats, and other animals that are not part of the natural ecosystem of the river, to come and live there. These animals carry diseases, which would not be kept within the confines of the dirty water. People who live near the stream or walk near it are the most likely to acquire the diseases, but they, in turn, could pass the germs on to other people they meet—people who don't pass by the river. Maybe people like you!

The beauty of clean water is not its only value. Clean water keeps our plants and animals healthy, our children healthy, and even YOU healthy. Please remember this editorial the next time you are too lazy to take your trash to the city dump.

Circle the letter of the best answer.

1. Which BEST describes the author's purpose for writing this editorial?

   A. to inform and entertain

   B. to persuade and inform

   C. to shock and awe

   D. to persuade and describe

2. The author tries to inform readers about

   A. children swimming in Snaky River.

   B. rat problems near the river.

   C. pollution in the river.

   D. contagious diseases.

3. The author tries to persuade people to

   A. avoid the polluted river.

   B. help keep the river clean.

   C. bring tires to the dump.

   D. swim in the river.

4. The fourth paragraph argues that

   A. the river is polluted.

   B. the river ecosystem is out of balance.

   C. a polluted river can get people sick.

   D. healthy people should avoid the river.

DIRECTIONS
Read the passage. Use the Reading Guide for tips that can help you interpret the author's purpose. Then answer the questions on the next page.

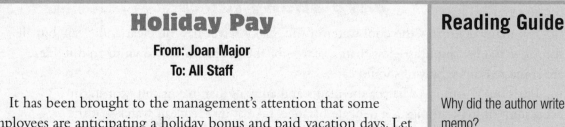

Holiday Pay

From: Joan Major
To: All Staff

It has been brought to the management's attention that some employees are anticipating a holiday bonus and paid vacation days. Let me be the first to let you all know that this will not be the case. There will be NO holiday bonus for any employee. Furthermore, there will be NO paid vacation days this holiday season.

The office will open and close at its usual business hours. There will be an end-of-day holiday party from 5:00 P.M. to 6:00 P.M. on December 20. Employees are encouraged to bring their own food and drink to the party as management will not provide any.

We are sorry for any inconvenience this may cause, but we trust that our employees will understand and do their best to work through these personal difficulties. As we all know, the team must always be placed before the individual.

Have a happy and productive 2008!

Sincerely,
Joan Major
Human Resources

Reading Guide

Why did the author write this memo?

....

Does the author use any entertaining or humorous elements?

....

What approach has the author used to get her point across?

Circle the letter of the best answer.

1. What is the author's purpose for writing this memo?

    A. to persuade employees to work harder

    B. to inform employees about holiday pay and vacation

    C. to wish employees a happy holiday season

    D. to describe the company's business practices

2. Why do you think the author scheduled the holiday party when she did?

    A. It is on a federal holiday.

    B. So it would not interfere with business hours.

    C. Employees requested it to be at this time.

    D. There is no paid vacation.

3. Which sentence from the memo is the most informative?

    A. "Let me be the first to let you all know that this will not be the case."

    B. "Have a happy and productive 2008!"

    C. "The office will open and close at its usual business hours."

    D. "There will be an end-of-day holiday party from 5:00 P.M. to 6:00 P.M. on December 20."

4. Based on the memo, what type of boss do you think Joan Major is?

    A. caring and responsible

    B. responsible and professional

    C. demanding and caring

    D. uncaring and demanding

DIRECTIONS
Read this poem. Then answer the questions on the next page.

The Song In The Dell

by Charles Carryl

1   I know a way
2   Of hearing what the larks and linnets say:
3   The larks tell of the sunshine and the sky;
4   The linnets from the hedges make reply,
5   And boast of hidden nests with mocking lay.
6   I know a way
7   Of keeping near the rabbits at their play:
8   They tell me of the cool and shady nooks
9   Where waterfalls disturb the placid brooks
10   That I may go and frolic in the spray.
11   I know a way
12   Of catching dewdrops on a night in May,
13   And threading them upon a spear of green,
14   That through their sides translucent may be seen
15   The sparkling hue that emeralds display.
16   I know a way
17   Of trapping sunbeams as they nimbly play
18   At hide-and-seek with meadow-grass and flowers,
19   And holding them in store for dreary hours
20   When winds are chill and all the sky is gray.
21   I know a way
22   Of stealing fragrance from the new-mown hay
23   And storing it in flasks of petals made,
24   To scent the air when all the flowers fade
25   And leave the woodland world to sad decay.
26   I know a way
27   Of coaxing snowflakes in their flight to stay
28   So still awhile, that, as they hang in air,
29   I weave them into frosty lace, to wear
30   About my head upon a sultry day.

Circle the letter of the best answer.

1. Read the following lines from the poem.

   "I know a way

   Of trapping sunbeams as they nimbly play

   At hide-and-seek with meadow-grass and flowers,

   And holding them in store for dreary hours

   When winds are chill and all the sky is gray."

   The author chose the language in this passage in order to

   A. persuade the reader.

   B. inform the reader.

   C. describe a feeling.

   D. tell a story.

2. The poem shows the author's belief that

   A. nature is beautiful.

   B. nature is dangerous.

   C. animals are happy.

   D. nature is harmless.

3. Which line from the poem is the MOST descriptive?

   A. line 1

   B. line 6

   C. line 9

   D. line 10

4. The language in the poem is BEST described as

   A. honest.

   B. angry.

   C. descriptive.

   D. persuasive.

5. The author MOST LIKELY

   A. traps sunbeams.

   B. plays with rabbits.

   C. coaxes snowflakes.

   D. loves the outdoors.

6. Which line from the poem is the least descriptive?

   A. line 26

   B. line 27

   C. line 28

   D. line 29

7. On a separate sheet of paper, write a short paragraph about the author's feelings toward nature. Use examples from the poem to support your response.

Lesson 2 • Main Idea and Details

A **main idea** is the most important idea in a paragraph or passage.

A **topic sentence** directly states the main idea in a paragraph.

Supporting details explain, describe, prove, or give examples about the main idea and topic sentence.

Example

Read this excerpt from a famous 1961 speech by President John F. Kennedy. Then answer the questions.

To the Moon

(1) I believe that this nation should commit itself to achieving the goal, before this decade is out, of landing a man on the moon and returning him safely to Earth. (2) No single space project in this period will be more impressive to mankind, or more important for the long-range exploration of space; and none will be so difficult or expensive to accomplish. (3) We propose to accelerate the development of the appropriate lunar space craft… (4) We propose additional funds for other engine development and for unmanned explorations—explorations which are particularly important for one purpose which this nation will never overlook: the survival of the man who first makes this daring flight. (5) But in a very real sense, it will not be one man going to the moon—if we make this judgment affirmatively, it will be an entire nation. (6) For all of us must work to put him there.

Circle the letter of the best answer.

1. What is the main idea of this passage?

    A. Wherever one American goes, all Americans go.

    B. The development of appropriate lunar space craft is too slow.

    C. President Kennedy wants an American to land on the moon and return to Earth.

    D. The nation should not overlook important safety concerns.

2. Which is the topic sentence?

    A. Sentence 1

    B. Sentence 2

    C. Sentence 3

    D. Sentence 4

DIRECTIONS
Read this passage about a newly discovered planet. Use the Reading Guide for tips. The tips can help you access prior knowledge and find the main idea and details as you read. Then answer the questions on the next page.

Gliese 581c

(1) Gliese 581c is a planet orbiting a sun 20 million light years away from Earth. (2) Some scientists believe it to be a "second Earth" that has the physical properties needed to support life as we know it.

(3) The planet, nicknamed Ymir, is the first rock planet besides Earth to orbit its sun in what scientists call the "habitable zone." (4) In theory, the habitable zone around a star is temperate enough for liquid water to exist. (5) Liquid water is a necessity for the existence of life as we know it. (6) This is why scientists are speculating about the possibilities of life on the distant Ymir.

(7) Ymir is believed to have a fairly moderate climate. (8) Scientists believe the surface temperature could range between 27 to 104 degrees Fahrenheit. (9) Water can exist without freezing or vaporizing in these temperatures. (10) This is similar to Earth's climate. (11) Earth's climate is great.

(12) Scientists' hypotheses about Ymir's climate are unproven though, because no direct measurements can be taken. (13) Theories do not take Ymir's atmosphere into consideration when estimating the temperature. (14) If Ymir has an atmosphere like Earth, the greenhouse effect could make the surface temperatures hotter.

(15) Ymir is also referred to as a "super-Earth." (16) It is about fifty percent bigger than our planet. (17) Its mass is nearly five times greater than Earth's.

(18) Ymir is difficult to study. (19) Scientists don't yet have the technology they need for detailed investigations. (20) Some astronomers believe it would be a good idea to send a satellite to the planet for further study. (21) That would help them learn more about this interesting newly discovered planet.

Reading Guide

What is the main idea of the passage?
....

What is the topic sentence in paragraph 2?
....

What details support the main idea in the last paragraph?

Circle the letter of the best answer.

1. What is the main idea of the first paragraph?

   A. Gliese 581c is a planet.

   B. Gliese 581c is 20 million light years away from Earth.

   C. Gliese 581c might support life.

   D. Gliese 581c orbits a sun.

2. What is the topic sentence in the last paragraph?

   A. Ymir is difficult to study.

   B. Scientists don't yet have the technology they need for detailed investigations.

   C. Some astronomers believe it would be a good idea to send a satellite to the planet for further study.

   D. That would help them learn more about this interesting newly discovered planet.

3. Which of the following details does NOT support the main idea in paragraph 3?

   A. Scientists believe the surface temperature could range between 27 to 104 degrees Fahrenheit.

   B. Water can exist without freezing or vaporizing in these temperatures.

   C. This is similar to Earth's climate.

   D. Earth's climate is great.

4. Which is a topic sentence?

   A. Liquid water is a necessity for the existence of life as we know it.

   B. Ymir is also referred to as a "super-Earth."

   C. Some astronomers believe it would be a good idea to send a satellite to the planet for further study.

   D. Theories do not take Ymir's atmosphere into consideration when estimating the temperature.

Step 2

You have learned that the main idea is the most important idea a writer offers in a passage. Details back up and support the main idea.

Details can be:

- examples that illustrate the main idea

- explanations that clarify the main idea

- descriptions that depict the main idea by appealing to one or more of the senses

- proof or evidence that backs up the main idea

- statistical data that supports the main idea

Example

Read the following passage. Look for clue words to help you find the main idea and supporting details.

LaKeisha's Trip

LaKeisha took a trip around much of the state of Indiana this summer, including Indianapolis and Columbus. Her family had decided they wanted to see as many historical landmarks as possible. In Indianapolis they toured the state capital, the Benjamin Harris home, and the World War Memorial. In Columbus, they visited the Miller house and the Irwin Union Bank building.

Fill in the diagram below to show your understanding of main idea and details. Place the main idea in the center circle and supporting details in the surrounding circles.

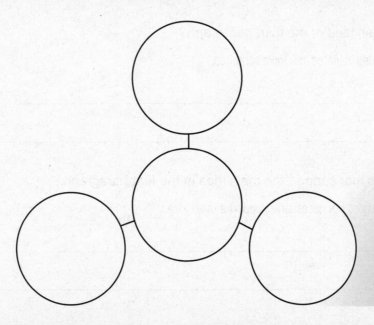

DIRECTIONS
Read this adaptation of President Dwight D. Eisenhower's January 17, 1961, farewell speech. Then use what you have learned about main idea and details to answer the questions. Make a graphic organizer on a separate sheet of paper to organize your thoughts.

Government must guard against the gain of needless influence by the military-industrial complex. The potential for the disastrous rise of misplaced power exists. This threat will persist. We must never let this pressure our liberties or democratic processes. We should take nothing for granted. Industrial and military machinery are needed to help us defend our peaceful goals. But security and liberty must prosper together. Citizens must stay alert. They must remain wise. They are the only ones who can ensure the proper mix of liberty and security.

The technological revolution in recent decades has brought many changes. It has shaped our industrial and military pursuits.

Research is at the center of this revolution. It has become more formalized, complex, and costly. Much research is done for the federal government. Independent inventors have been passed by teams of scientists. Research is expensive. Pursuit of government contracts has replaced intellectual curiosity. For every old blackboard, there are hundreds of new computers.

We don't want our nation's scholars to get obsessed with federal contracts. The power of money is a serious danger to independent research.

1. What is the main idea of the first paragraph?

   HINT: The main idea is the most important idea.

   _____

   _____

2. What is the main idea of the third paragraph?

   HINT: The main idea is stated in a topic sentence.

   _____

   _____

3. List two details that support the main idea in the first paragraph.

   HINT: An opinion does not necessarily support a main idea.

   _____

   _____

DIRECTIONS
Read this excerpt about classes in society. Then answer the questions.

adapted and excerpted from

The Communist Manifesto (1848)

by Karl Marx and Friedrich Engels

In the earlier periods of history, we find that, almost everywhere, society has been arranged into various complicated orders, a hierarchy of social rank. In ancient Rome, we have aristocrats, knights, working class, and slaves. In the Middle Ages, we find land owners, land renters, master craftspeople, assistant craftspeople, students, and servants. In almost all of these orders, we see higher and lower classes.

The modern capitalist society that has sprouted from the ruins of the Middle Ages has not done away with class rivalries. It has only established new classes, new forms of oppression, and new struggles in place of old ones. Our age, the age of the capitalists, has this distinct feature: It has simplified the class rivalries. Our society as a whole is increasingly splitting up into two great hostile camps, into two great classes that directly face each other: the owners and the workers.

Circle the letter of the best answer.

1. What is the main idea of this passage?

   A. Modern society has done away with the class-based structure.

   B. Every society has been arranged by class.

   C. The Middle Ages system has been ruined.

   D. Our age has simplified class rivalries.

2. The first paragraph mainly includes which type of supporting detail?

   A. example

   B. explanation

   C. description

   D. proof

3. What does the reader learn from the details in the second paragraph?

   A. Modern society is structured the same way ancient Rome was.

   B. We are living in the Middle Ages.

   C. Modern society is just a new form of class-based structure.

   D. There are no more struggles in modern society.

4. Which type of supporting detail is the last sentence?

   A. example

   B. explanation

   C. description

   D. proof

DIRECTIONS
Read the passage. Use the Reading Guide for tips that can help you analyze the main idea and details as you read. Then answer the questions on the next page.

adapted and excerpted from

Dream Psychology (1899)

by Sigmund Freud

In what we may call "pre-scientific days," people had definite ideas about how to interpret dreams. When they were recalled after waking, dreams were thought of as either friendly or hostile messages from some higher power. With the rise of scientific thought, the job of interpreting dreams was transferred from mythology to psychology. Today, nearly all educated people believe dreams are products of the dreamer's own mind.

However, since the downfall of the mythological view of dreams, a systematic interpretation of the dream has been lacking. Many problems, such as the origin of the dream; its relationship to our waking life; its lack or response to outside stimuli; its many characteristics that go against our waking thoughts; the difference between dream images and the feelings they bring about; the way in which, upon waking, we regard the dream as something bizarre; and the way the dream almost immediately begins to escape memory upon waking, have all lacked satisfactory answers for many hundreds of years. The most important question, that of the meaning of the dream, is a double-sided one. First, there is the psychological significance of the dream—what is its relationship to other psychological and biological processes? Second, there is the dream's meaning—can sense be made of each single dream the way it can of other mental processes?

Reading Guide

What does the topic sentence tell the reader the first paragraph will be about?

Is the second sentence a descriptive supporting detail? Why or why not?

What is the main idea of the second paragraph?

How does the main idea of the first paragraph relate to the main idea of the second paragraph?

The second paragraph mainly includes which type of supporting detail?

Circle the letter of the best answer.

1. Which is the topic sentence of the first paragraph?

   A. In what we may call "prescientific days," people had definite ideas about how to interpret dreams.

   B. When they were recalled after waking, dreams were thought of as either friendly or hostile messages from some higher power.

   C. With the rise of scientific thought, the job of interpreting dreams was transferred from mythology to psychology.

   D. Today, nearly all educated people believe dreams are products of the dreamer's own mind.

2. Why does Freud include the second sentence of the first paragraph?

   A. to give a specific instance of the main idea

   B. to clarify the main idea

   C. to depict the main idea through sensory detail

   D. to give evidence that backs up the main idea

3. What does the main idea of the second paragraph tell the reader what Freud will present in *Dream Psychology*?

   A. He will describe a system for making dreams more vivid.

   B. He will show how dreams are harmful.

   C. He will show how dreams are helpful.

   D. He will describe a system for dream interpretation.

4. What is the main idea of the passage?

   A. Dreams are messages from a higher power.

   B. A modern, scientific system for dream interpretation is needed.

   C. Ideas that come in dreams are the opposite of waking ideas.

   D. Dreams are useless and should be ignored.

5. How do the details in the second sentence of the second paragraph relate to its main idea?

   A. They illustrate the main idea.

   B. They clarify the main idea.

   C. They give sensory information about the main idea.

   D. They give evidence that proves the main idea.

DIRECTIONS
Read this passage. Then answer the questions on the next page.

adapted and excerpted from

The Starry Messenger (1610)

by Galileo Galilei

The things I will propose in this short essay to all students of nature are great indeed. I say great because the subject itself is excellent, the things I propose are completely new and unexpected, and these things have been revealed to our senses by a new and exciting instrument.

It is surely a great thing to increase the number of visible unmoving stars by adding countless more that were unimagined before and exposing ten times the number of familiar stars.

It is a very beautiful and gratifying thing to see the body of the moon, which is at a distance from us equal to sixty times the radius of Earth, as if it were only two times Earth's radius from us. This makes it appear thirty times larger than when viewed by the naked eye. In this way, we learn that the moon is not robed in a smooth and polished surface, but is in fact rough and uneven, covered everywhere, like Earth's surface, with mountains, valleys, and chasms.

It also seems to me a matter of no small importance to end the dispute about the Milky Way, by making it available to the senses as well as the intellect. Similarly, it will be a pleasant and elegant thing to show that the nature of those stars which astronomers have previously called "nebulous" is far different from what has been believed up until now. Of course, what is most wondrous, and what especially moves us to seek the attention of all astronomers and philosophers, is the discovery of four wandering stars that have never been observed before. Like Venus and Mercury, which have their own orbits around the sun, these newly-discovered stars orbit around a certain already-known star.

I have discovered and observed all of these facts not many days ago with the help of a spyglass, which I, myself, devised. Perhaps even more remarkable things will be discovered in time by me or other observers with the help of such an instrument.

Circle the letter of the best answer.

1. How does Galileo achieve his new discoveries?

   A. with a long ladder

   B. with a new telescope

   C. with superpowers

   D. with a little help from his friends

2. In which paragraph is the main idea of the passage MOST clearly revealed?

   A. paragraph 1

   B. paragraph 3

   C. paragraph 4

   D. paragraph 5

3. What is the main idea of the passage?

   A. The telescope is a pointless item that no student of nature needs.

   B. Galileo has visited the moon and several stars in the Milky Way.

   C. The discoveries made with the telescope are important and exciting.

   D. Galileo is a great inventor but does not want to share his inventions.

4. Which type of details does Galileo mainly give about the moon?

   A. example

   B. explanation

   C. description

   D. proof

5. The fourth paragraph reveals that "nebulous" stars

   A. are like Venus and Mercury.

   B. orbit the Milky Way.

   C. are not what people thought.

   D. are not very colorful.

6. Galileo believes that the planets revolve around

   A. Venus.

   B. Mercury.

   C. Earth.

   D. the sun.

7. What is the main idea of the third paragraph?

   A. Upon closer inspection, the moon is made of cheese.

   B. Upon closer inspection, the moon looks much like Earth.

   C. The moon looks the same close up as it does from far away.

   D. The moon is much larger than Earth.

8. On a separate sheet of paper, explain the main idea of the fourth paragraph and identify which type(s) of supporting details Galileo gives.

Lesson 3 • Context Clues

Step 1

A **context clue** is a word or phrase near an unknown word that helps the reader understand its meaning. A **definition** is one type of context clue. Read the following sentence:

> We went out in a small boat, also called a *dinghy.*

The phrase *also called* tells the reader that the definition of *dinghy* is "a small boat."

An **antonym** is a word that means the opposite of another word. This is another type of context clue. Read the following sentence:

> Phil finds reality television *captivating,* unlike Jerry, who finds it boring.

The word *unlike* tells the reader that *captivating* means "interesting" because it is opposite of *boring.*

Example

Read this passage about the English writer George Eliot. Then answer the questions.

George Eliot

Mary Anne Evans was a writer, much better known by her pseudonym, or false name, George Eliot. Evans most likely chose the man's name George so that the readers of her time would take her work more seriously. In her sixty-one years, Eliot wrote many poems, novels, and works of nonfiction. Her most famous work is a novel called *Silas Marner.*

Circle the letter of the best answer.

1. What does *pseudonym* mean?

    A. written work

    B. nonfiction writer

    C. false name

    D. man's name

2. What word tells you that a novel is fiction?

    A. poems

    B. nonfiction

    C. sixty-one

    D. wrote

DIRECTIONS
Read this passage about nervousness. Use the Reading Guide for tips. The tips can help you use context clues to find the meaning of unknown words. Then answer the questions on the next page.

adapted and excerpted from

Outwitting Our Nerves: A Primer of Psychotherapy (1921)

by Josephine A. Jackson, M.D. and Helen M. Salisbury

(1) Many people would resent being called anything but normal. (2) These same people are not at all loath, which means unwilling, to be thought of as "different," when it comes to small details. (3) For example, how many of us don't go to much effort to hide the fact that we "didn't sleep a wink last night" or that we "can't stand" a ticking clock or a crowing rooster? (4) We sometimes think it is a mark of distinction, instead of shame, to have a fragile stomach and to have to choose our food carefully.

(5) If we are honest with ourselves, some of us will have to admit that our own ailments, or medical problems, seem quite interesting. (6) Yet, another person's ills are "simply nervous," imaginary, or abnormal. (7) After all, many of us have a degree of nervousness.

Reading Guide

What phrase in sentence 2 signals a context clue?

Which kind of context clue tells you what *distinction* means?

Which word in sentence 5 signals a context clue?

Circle the letter of the best answer.

1. What does *loath* mean in sentence 2?

   A. same

   B. different

   C. willing

   D. unwilling

2. What does *distinction* mean in sentence 4?

   A. shame

   B. pride

   C. fragile

   D. food

3. Which word or phrase signals a context clue for the word *distinction*?

   A. sometimes

   B. mark of

   C. instead of

   D. have to

4. What are *ailments?*

   A. medical problems

   B. family problems

   C. beverages

   D. medical cures

You have learned that a context clue is a word or phrase that helps the reader find the meaning of an unknown word. A context clue can be a definition or an antonym. A context clue can also be

- a **synonym**, which is a word that has a similar meaning to another word.

  Denny *abhors,* or hates, messiness.

- an example.

  Every superhero needs a *retreat,* such as a secret hideout.

- a comparison or contrast.

  Liz has an *infatuation* with video games, but they don't interest me at all.

- a cause or effect.

  The car's *din* was awful because it had no muffler.

Example

Read the following passage about the universe. Look for context clues that help you find the meaning of unknown words.

adapted and excerpted from

On the Revolutions of Heavenly Spheres (1543)

by Nicolaus Copernicus

The sun is the middle of everything. The universe is a beautiful temple. Who would place the sun anywhere other than the spot where it can light the entire temple at once? This is why some people have called the sun the lantern of the universe. Others have called it the mind. Still, others say it is the ruler of the universe. The sun governs the family of planets that revolves, or turns, around it.

Earth is not deprived of the moon. On the contrary, the moon is always with it. Aristotle says the moon has an extremely close kinship with Earth, such as a daughter has with her mother.

Fill in the diagram below to show your understanding of context clues.

Unknown Word	Kind of Context Clue	Meaning of Word
revolves	synonym	
deprived		left without
kinship		

DIRECTIONS
Read this adaptation of Friedrich Nietzsche's philosophy. Then use what you have learned to use context clues to define unknown words. Make a graphic organizer on a separate sheet of paper to organize your thoughts.

adapted and excerpted from

Beyond Good and Evil (1886)

by Friedrich Nietzsche

Very few people can be truly independent. To do so, one must be strong. Anyone who tries to be independent without being obliged, such as a social outcast is, proves to be very daring. This daring person enters into a labyrinth, or maze. He or she adds to the dangers that life already brings. No one can see how and where the independent person loses his or her way, becomes cut off, and is torn apart by some monster of right and wrong. If something bad happens to the independent person, the average person cannot understand it. The average person cannot feel it or sympathize. The independent person can never return to the company of average people. He or she can never get that sympathy back again.

1. Which type of context clue helps you define *obliged*? How do you know?

   HINT: Words like *such as* or *for example* are clue words.

   _____

   _____

2. What does *obliged* mean?

   HINT: Reread the sentence and look for clues.

   _____

   _____

3. What word signals a context clue for *labyrinth*? Which type of context clue is this?

   HINT: Reread the sentence and look at the words before and after *labyrinth*.

   _____

   _____

Step 3

DIRECTIONS
Read this excerpt about a scientific discovery. Then answer the questions.

Eight-Foot Scorpion

by Ellen Pogri

British scientists have found remains of a 400-million-year-old sea scorpion in Germany. They say it is the biggest bug ever found. The scorpion is thought to be over eight feet long.

These scorpions were able to survive because they had no equal enemies. They were able to get so big because the air 400 million years ago had much more oxygen than it does today.

Once vertebrates, or animals with backbones, grew larger and became successful predators, the giant sea scorpions became extinct. One reason is that the scorpions had to shed their hard outer shells, also called exoskeletons, to grow. This left them vulnerable, or defenseless, to attack. The scorpions had to shrink over time to avoid these attacks.

These ancient sea scorpions are believed to be the ancestors of all modern arthropods, such as spiders, scorpions, insects, lobsters, and crabs.

Circle the letter of the best answer.

1. Which kind of context clue tells you what *vertebrates* are?

   A. compare or contrast

   B. cause or effect

   C. definition

   D. example

2. What are *exoskeletons*?

   A. former skeletons

   B. internal bones

   C. soft outer bones

   D. hard outer shells

3. Which word signals a context clue for *vulnerable*?

   A. left

   B. them

   C. or

   D. to

4. Which of the following is NOT an *arthropod*?

   A. lobster

   B. bird

   C. spider

   D. insect

DIRECTIONS
Read the passage. Use the Reading Guide for tips that can help you use context clues to help you define unknown words as you read. Then answer the questions on the next page.

adapted and excerpted from

Six Years in the Prisons of England

(1869)

by a merchant

The major thing that happened while I was in prison in Scotland was a conspiracy, or plan, among the prisoners to escape. The plan was disclosed to a number of prisoners, but they did not tell me about it. One prisoner made lock-picking tools out of pieces of his bed to open the cell doors.

The plan went like this: One of the older prisoners was known to have seizures, which are fits of spasms. He was going to fake one so the night officer would have to go to his cell to help him. Then, instead of facilitating the officer, the old man's cellmate would stop the officer and "put his lights out." This would give the man with the tools a chance to pick the cell locks.

The whole plan was thwarted because another prisoner heard about the plan and told the officers. The next morning, the cells were searched, and the lock-picking tools were found.

Reading Guide

Which kind of context clue tells you what *conspiracy* means?

....

What does *disclosed* mean?

....

Which kind of context clue tells you what *seizures* are?

....

What phrase signals a context clue for *facilitating*?

....

What does *thwarted* mean?

Circle the letter of the best answer.

1. What is a *conspiracy*?

   A. a major thing

   B. a prison

   C. a plan

   D. a tool

2. Which kind of context clue tells you what *disclosed* means?

   A. compare or contrast

   B. cause or effect

   C. definition

   D. example

3. What are *seizures*?

   A. old prisoners

   B. fits of spasms

   C. plans

   D. lock-picking tools

4. What does *facilitating* mean?

   A. escaping

   B. faking

   C. stopping

   D. helping

5. Which word signals a context clue for *thwarted*?

   A. another

   B. because

   C. whole

   D. about

DIRECTIONS
Read this passage. Then answer the questions on the next page.

adapted and excerpted from

Incidents in the Life of a Slave Girl (1861)

by Harriet A. Jacobs

I had been with the new family for only a few weeks. Another slave was brought to the workhouse and tied to the joist, which is a beam that holds the building up. The slave was tied by his arms so his feet dangled above the floor. I will never forget that night. I had never heard hundreds of blows fall on a human being. His piteous, or miserable, cries of "Oh, pray don't do it!" rang in my ears for months afterward.

There were many conjectures as to the cause of this terrible punishment. Some said Master accused the man of stealing corn. Others said the man had claimed that his wife's baby was really the master's son. The man and his wife were both black, but the child was very fair. A few months later, the master sold the man and his wife to a slave trader.

Slaves were often persecuted, or mistreated, by people other than the master. I once saw a slave girl dying after giving birth. She cried out in pain. Instead of being kind or helping her, the master's wife mocked her.

She said to the slave girl, "Do you suffer? I am glad! You deserve it all and more too."

Circle the letter of the best answer.

1. Which type of context clue helps you define *joist?*

    A. antonym

    B. definition

    C. synonym

    D. compare or contrast

2. Which word is a synonym of *piteous?*

    A. cries

    B. blows

    C. miserable

    D. afterward

3. Which word is an antonym of *fair?*

    A. white

    B. black

    C. child

    D. both

4. What does *fair* mean in this passage?

    A. black

    B. slow

    C. pale

    D. obese

5. What does *persecuted* mean?

    A. befriended

    B. helped

    C. whipped

    D. mistreated

6. Which type of context clue helps you define *mocked?*

    A. antonym

    B. definition

    C. synonym

    D. compare or contrast

7. What does *mocked* mean?

    A. was kind

    B. was cruel

    C. helped

    D. pretended

8. On a separate sheet of paper, define *conjectures,* and list two context clues that helped you find its definition.

Lesson 4 • Figurative Language

Step 1

Figurative language does not mean what it actually says. Writers use figurative language to present ideas in fresh and unusual ways.

The chart describes four types of figurative language:

Type of Figurative Language	Definition	Example
simile	a comparison between two unlike things using *like* or *as*	Her words are as stimulating as a fresh cup of coffee.
metaphor	a comparison between two unlike things that does not use *like* or *as*	That test was a beast and a half.
hyperbole	an extreme exaggeration	I've been waiting for the bus forever.
idiom	a phrase that means something different from its literal meaning; often particular to a region or group of people	Ted took his offer off the table.

Example

Read this excerpt from a play. Then answer the questions.

Macbeth (c. 1603)

by William Shakespeare

Life's but a walking shadow; a poor player,
That struts and frets his hour upon the stage,
And then is heard no more: it is a tale
Told by an idiot, full of sound and fury,
Signifying nothing.

Circle the letter of the best answer.

1. "Life's but a walking shadow" is an example of

    A. a simile.

    B. a metaphor.

    C. an idiom.

    D. a hyperbole.

2. A "walking shadow" is a metaphor for

    A. a poor player.

    B. a tale told by an idiot.

    C. an hour upon the stage.

    D. life.

DIRECTIONS
Read the story. Use the Reading Guide for tips. The tips can help you access prior knowledge about figurative language as you read. Then answer the questions on the next page.

Escaping the Storm

(1) We'd been glued to the TV for days. (2) We knew it was coming—a Category 5 hurricane as wide as a mountain range that was howling like a demon. (3) The storm had already pounded Florida, killing more than a dozen people. (4) Now it was barreling across the Gulf of Mexico, a one-eyed sea monster heading straight for our city.

(5) The newscasters said we had to evacuate, but some of our neighbors weren't budging. (6) "New Orleans is my home, and we've seen plenty of storms before," one said. (7) "I'll just sit tight and keep my fingers crossed." (8) Besides, some said, where else could they go?

(9) My dad said we couldn't risk it. (10) We didn't have a car, so we'd have to pile into our uncle's truck—six of us altogether—and drive to our grandparents up in Shreveport. (11) They were a million miles north, but they weren't on the coast, like us.

(12) The storm was getting closer. (13) It was a race against the clock. (14) Dad told my sister and me to pack one week's worth of clothes. (15) Then he told us to go through the house and take the few things we valued most. (16) How can you decide something like that?

(17) I stared at my room—at my posters, my photos, my music, my life. (18) I was shaking like lost a child in the cold. (19) For sixteen years I'd lived there. (20) In a heartbeat it could all be gone. (21) Suddenly everything we owned was a treasure.

(22) Dad came and touched my shoulder. (23) He said we had to go. (24) We didn't know then that Katrina would be the third-strongest hurricane in U.S. history. (25) We didn't know our levees would break like popsicle sticks, leaving 80 percent of our city flooded. (26) We didn't know nearly two thousand people were about to lose their lives.

(27) We only knew we had to say goodbye and hoped it wasn't forever.

Reading Guide

The narrator is not literally "glued to the TV" in sentence 1. This is an example of a metaphor. Underline any other metaphors in the passage.

In sentences 2 and 4, which unlike things does the author compare? What images do these comparisons create?

What does the phrase "race against the clock" in sentence 13 mean? Why does the narrator use this phrase? Put a check mark above the other idioms in the story.

Circle the four similes in this story.

Circle the letter of the best answer.

1. In sentence 7, what does the idiom "keep your fingers crossed" mean?

    A. stand very still

    B. forget about everything

    C. hope to be lucky

    D. get angry

2. The writer compares which two unlike things using a simile?

    A. the newscasters and the neighbors

    B. the hurricane and a mountain range

    C. New Orleans and Shreveport

    D. photos and a heartbeat

3. Which of these is a metaphor for the hurricane?

    A. a lost child in the cold

    B. a stubborn neighbor

    C. an abandoned house

    D. a one-eyed sea monster

4. How does the narrator use hyperbole when talking about traveling to Shreveport?

    A. by saying it is not on the coast

    B. by saying it is a million miles north

    C. by saying they had to save one or two things they valued

    D. by saying they did not have a car

You have learned that figurative language uses non-literal meaning. It is used to present ideas in fresh and unusual ways.

Review these examples of figurative language:

- simile: That new song is hot like soup.

- metaphor: That rookie is greener than wasabi.

- hyperbole: Her voice is so beautiful it could make a grown man cry.

- idiom: I don't want to say for sure; let's play it by ear.

Example

Read the following passage, adapted from Joseph Conrad's *Heart of Darkness* (1902). Look for figurative language that helps describe the scene.

> The Thames stretched before us like the beginning of an endless waterway. The sea and the sky were one piece, welded together without a joint. In the evening light, the tanned sails of the barges drifting with the tide seemed to stand still in red clusters, occasionally gleaming. There was a haze on the low shores that ran out to sea in vanishing flatness. The air was dark above Gravesend, behind us. Farther back still, a mournful gloom hung over the biggest, and the greatest, town on Earth.

Fill in the chart below to show your understanding of figurative language. Write one example of each type (simile, metaphor, hyperbole, and idiom) from the passage above into the chart below.

Type of Figurative Language	Example
simile	
metaphor	
hyperbole	
idiom	

DIRECTIONS
Read this adaptation from Nathaniel Hawthorne's *Young Goodman Brown* (1835). Then use what you have learned about figurative language to answer the questions. Make a graphic organizer on a separate sheet of paper to organize your thoughts.

The cry of grief, rage, and terror was yet piercing the night, when the unhappy husband held his breath for a response. There was a scream, drowned immediately in a louder murmur of voices, fading into far-off laughter, as the dark cloud swept away, leaving the clear and silent sky above Goodman Brown. But something fluttered lightly down through the air and caught on the branch of a tree. The young man seized it, and beheld a pink ribbon.

"My Faith is gone!" cried he, after one stupefied moment. "There is no good on earth; and sin is but a name. Come, devil; for to thee is this world given."

And, maddened with despair, so that he laughed loud and long, did Goodman Brown grasp his staff and set forth again, at such a rate that he seemed to fly along the forest path rather than to walk or run. The road grew wilder and drearier and more faintly traced, and vanished at length, leaving him in the heart of the dark wilderness, still rushing onward with the instinct that guides mortal man to evil. The whole forest was peopled with frightful sounds—the creaking of the trees, the howling of wild beasts, and the yell of Indians; while sometimes the wind tolled like a distant church bell, and sometimes gave a broad roar around the traveler, as if all Nature were laughing him to scorn. But he was himself the chief horror of the scene, and shrank not from its other horrors.

"Ha! ha! ha!" roared Goodman Brown when the wind laughed at him.

1. What effect does Hawthorne's use of figurative language have on the reader?

    HINT: What types of figurative language does Hawthorne use? Why?

2. Find an example of an idiom from the story and describe what it means.

    HINT: An idiom is an expression common to a certain region or culture. It is not meant be taken literally.

3. Find an example of a simile from the passage and describe what it means.

    HINT: A simile makes a comparison using *like* or *as*.

Step 3

DIRECTIONS
Read this passage about the Internet. Then answer the questions.

Get Connected

My Internet connection used to be so slow! It was like a tank being pushed up a hill by my grandmother. For too long, we had only a dial-up connection at my house. It was awful! I would get frustrated every time. It took half my life to download one song. I didn't know how I dealt with it.

My parents barely used the Internet, so it didn't really bother them. I asked them again and again to get a broadband connection, but they refused. My father just said it was unnecessary. My mother said I should be spending more time doing my homework and less time playing on the Internet. I was finally able to change their minds by convincing them that a broadband connection would enable me to go the extra mile in school.

Now everything I want to do on the Internet is painless. I can listen to my favorite songs and watch hilarious videos. Everything is at my fingertips. Our new connection is a Formula One racecar driven by Michael Schumacher in the Grand Prix. I love it!

Circle the letter of the best answer.

1. How does the writer use a simile in the first paragraph?

   A. to compare a dial-up connection to a song

   B. to compare a dial-up connection to a tank

   C. to compare a tank to a grandmother

   D. to compare grandmother to a hill

2. What does the author mean by the sentence, "It took half my life to download one song"?

   A. The author wants to be twice as old as she is.

   B. The author wants downloads to take as long.

   C. The author thinks downloads take too long.

   D. The author wants to be half as old as she is.

3. The expression "go the extra mile" means

   A. do more than is required.

   B. the school is a mile too far.

   C. the author will enter a race.

   D. travel as far as one can.

4. What does the metaphor in the third paragraph mean?

   A. Michael Schumacher installs broadband connections.

   B. A broadband connection is extremely fast.

   C. Michael Schumacher drives with his fingertips.

   D. The author loves to watch the Grand Prix.

DIRECTIONS
Read the story. Use the Reading Guide for tips that can help you interpret figurative language as you read. Then answer the questions on the next page.

Sky Bus

Berlia trudged apprehensively down the elevated tunnel that led to the plane door. She had never been inside a plane in her life, and she felt like a tiny mouse heading toward the open mouth of a cat. The closer she got to the door, the more her feet seemed to weigh. She estimated them to be three thousand pounds each.

Berlia had good reason to be frightened. Her grandfather had flown planes in World War II, and she had heard him tell many stories about planes crashing and pilots having to bail out.

Not only was Berlia flying for the first time, but she was doing it alone. This double whammy was, of course, making it all seem worse. She was going to visit her aunt and uncle for part of summer vacation, but her mother had to work. So, here was Berlia, alone, about to enter this sleeping dragon and not feeling at all reassured by the smiles of the stranger in the flight attendant uniform next to her.

Finally, she stepped into the plane itself. It looked a lot like a bus inside—aisles, seats, overhead luggage compartments. She calmed herself by pretending that she was, indeed, in a bus. She was able to maintain this illusion until the dragon suddenly awoke and leapt from the Earth.

Despite Berlia's fear, the flight was uneventful. Still, she couldn't have been more relieved when the plane touched down two hours later. As soon as the plane door opened, Berlia bolted, like a mare freed from a week-long captivity in a pen, and didn't stop running until she found the arms of her uncle.

Reading Guide

Why does the author compare Berlia to a mouse?

How does the author make use of hyperbole in the first paragraph?

Explain the idiom in the third paragraph.

To what does the author compare the plane more than once in the passage?

How would a mare feel after being trapped in a pen for a week?

Circle the letter of the best answer.

1. Which of the following would mean the same as the simile in the first paragraph?

   A. like a dog heading toward the open mouth of a cat

   B. like a goldfish swimming toward the open mouth of a shark

   C. like a seagull flying toward the open mouth of a mosquito

   D. like a lion heading toward the open mouth of an elephant

2. What does the hyperbole in the first paragraph mean?

   A. Berlia needs a new pair of shoes.

   B. Berlia has two broken legs.

   C. Each step toward the plane is difficult.

   D. Gravity is stronger near the plane.

3. Which of the following has a similar meaning to the idiom in the third paragraph?

   A. a one-two punch

   B. a double exposure

   C. one bitten, twice shy

   D. a double-decker bus

4. Why does the author compare the plane to a dragon?

   A. Dragons can fly and breathe fire.

   B. Dragons are large and have treasure.

   C. Dragons are scary and have scales.

   D. Dragons are scary and can fly.

5. Why does the author compare Berlia to a mare in the last paragraph?

   A. She loves to ride horses.

   B. She looks like a horse.

   C. Her uncle is a rancher.

   D. She is excited to be free.

DIRECTIONS
Read this story about a poetry slam. Then answer the questions on the next page.

Slam to Success

I feel like a child tossing and turning on the night before her first day at school. Indeed, tomorrow is a big day. My two best friends and I are going to wake up early, drive three hours to Columbus, Ohio, and compete in a Poetry Slam. A Poetry Slam is a competition in which many poets gather together to recite their poems out loud in front of an audience. The poems are judged by a panel of experts, who pick a first-, a second-, and a third-place winner. I've been preparing for this since the day I was born. My mom said my first cries were poetry to her ears.

Yesterday my friends and I got together for a dry run. We each read the poem we chose for the competition. This is the one I have chosen:

> For a thousand nights, I have barked upon your front porch.
> I'm a rabid Doberman Pinscher guarding your innocence,
> Foaming in the sapphire wind that winds around my neck
> Like a foggy dry ice scarf.
>
> For a thousand days, I have warded off nightmare intruders.
> I'm a dog sitting in a catbird seat, ready to pounce
> On empty suitors who fall like lemmings
> Into your sacred lap.

I cannot wait until we get to Columbus. With a poem that outstanding and original, I'm bound to take the grand prize. I will be recognized throughout the world as the premier bard of our time. Move over Shakespeare!

Circle the letter of the best answer.

1. How does a child MOST LIKELY feel on the night before the first day of school?

    A. angry

    B. relaxed

    C. tired

    D. nervous

2. Why does the narrator say she has been preparing since birth?

    A. She has worked long and hard.

    B. She was just born yesterday.

    C. She does not know when she was born.

    D. She learned to talk before birth.

3. Explain the metaphor the narrator's mother uses.

    A. She likes the sound of any child's crying.

    B. Her daughter's first sounds meant a lot to her.

    C. She needs to have her hearing checked.

    D. She does not know what poetry sounds like.

4. How does the speaker use hyperbole in the poem?

    A. to express a precise length of time

    B. to indicate a great devotion to the subject

    C. to show an ability to count very high

    D. to express a great sense of boredom

5. Why does the speaker choose the Doberman Pinscher for the metaphor in the second line of the poem?

    A. Dobermans are cute and cuddly.

    B. Dobermans love front porches.

    C. Dobermans are strong and alert.

    D. Dobermans are lazy and fat.

6. Why is the wind "like a foggy dry ice scarf" in the poem?

    A. The wind feels cold on the speaker's neck.

    B. The wind is made of frozen water.

    C. The wind is often used in science experiments.

    D. The speaker dresses in dry-ice clothing.

7. What does the speaker of the poem mean by comparing the suitors to lemmings?

    A. The suitors are fuzzy rodents.

    B. The suitors are happy-go-lucky.

    C. The suitors eat grass and leaves.

    D. The suitors are mindless followers.

8. On a separate sheet of paper, identify the two idioms in the passage, and explain what each means.

Lesson 5 • Chronological Order

Chronological order is the sequence in which things happen. Chronological order tells what happens first, next, and last.

Writers use chronological order as a way to organize their writing. Many narratives, for example, are organized in the order in which events occur. Chronological order is also used to show steps in a process or in a set of instructions. It is important that such steps be listed in the correct order so that they are clear to readers.

Example

Read this passage. Then answer the questions below.

Humans in Space

The early history of human space travel is fascinating. The first person to go into space was the Russian cosmonaut Yuri Gagarin. In April, 1961, he made one orbit around Earth in a spacecraft. The next person in space was the American astronaut Alan Shepard. He traveled in space in May, 1961, but he did not orbit Earth. In February, 1962, 10 months after Shepard's spaceflight, astronaut John Glenn made the first U.S. orbit around Earth. Cosmonaut Valentina Tereshkova became the first woman in space in June, 1963. She spent nearly three days in space and orbited Earth 48 times.

Circle the letter of the best answer.

1. Which of these events happened first?

   A. John Glenn orbited Earth.

   B. Yuri Gagarin orbited Earth.

   C. Alan Shepard went into space.

   D. Valentina Tereshkova went into space.

2. When did the second human spaceflight occur?

   A. April, 1961

   B. May, 1961

   C. February, 1962

   D. June, 1963

DIRECTIONS
Read this narrative about a frightening attack at sea and a young teen's recovery. Use the Reading Guide for tips on identifying chronological order.

Attack and Recovery

(1) For Bethany Hamilton, October 31, 2003, was a day that changed her life forever. A prize-winning surfer since early grade school, the young 13-year-old from Hawaii paddled out into the ocean on her surfboard that Halloween morning. She could have never imagined what was about to happen.

(2) At about 7 A.M., Bethany was lying on her surfboard with her left arm in the water. Suddenly, a 14-foot tiger shark attacked her, biting through her board and tearing off her left arm, just inches below her shoulder.

(3) After the attack, Bethany paddled to the shore using her right arm. Her best friend and her friend's father, who were surfing with her, created a tourniquet using a surfboard leash and tied it around the remaining part of her left arm. Then they rushed her to the hospital. She had lost over 60 percent of her blood and needed several surgeries.

(4) Bethany was determined not to let the attack end her dream of becoming a professional surfer. Less than a month after the attack, she was back on her board. She slowly taught herself to surf with one arm, and she began competing again. Just eight months after losing her arm, she came in fifth in a national surfing championship.

(5) The year following the attack, Bethany was given a special Courage Award at the Teen Choice Awards. She also wrote an autobiography called *Soul Surfer*. Three years later, a short documentary film, *Heart of a Soul Surfer*, was made based on her story.

(6) Today, Bethany is still competing—and winning first-place prizes. She is one of the top female surfers in the world. She receives countless letters and e-mails from fans and well wishers around the world who are inspired by her courage, determination, and positive attitude.

Reading Guide

What is the first thing Bethany did on October 31, 2003?

What happened right after the shark attacked?

What two phrases in paragraph 4 help explain the order of events?

When was the documentary film made? Was it before or after her book came out?

Circle the letter of the best answer.

1. Which of these events happened first on October 31, 2003?

    A. Bethany was attacked by a shark.

    B. Bethany was rushed to the hospital.

    C. Bethany paddled out into the ocean on her surfboard.

    D. Bethany had a tourniquet tied around the top of her left arm.

2. What happened less than a month after the shark attack?

    A. Bethany wrote an autobiography called *Soul Surfer*.

    B. Bethany got back on her surfboard.

    C. Bethany came in fifth in a national surfing championship.

    D. A short documentary film was made based on Bethany's story.

3. When was Bethany given a special Courage Award?

    A. less than a month after the attack

    B. three years after the attack

    C. the year following the attack

    D. the day before the attack

4. Which of these phrases does NOT indicate chronological order?

    A. *Three years later…*

    B. *After the attack…*

    C. *Just eight months after…*

    D. *She receives countless letters…*

Step 2

Clue words such as *next* or *today* will help you keep track of sequence and time order in a passage. Study these clue words:

Clue Words	
Words Showing Sequence	*first, second, next, before, after, then, while, lastly, finally, in the end*
Words Showing Time	*now, today, soon, next week, in a month, a year later, over time, by the time*

Example

Now read the following passage. Look for clue words that show chronological order.

A Whirlwind Tour

I can't wait for our trip to San Francisco. My sister and I have it all planned out. The first thing we'll do is visit the Golden Gate Bridge. It's nearly two miles long, but we're going to walk across it. After that, we'll explore Golden Gate Park. It has gardens, lakes and a Japanese tea garden. Then we'll head to Market Street, where we can catch a cable car. We *have* to ride on a cable car. We've been looking forward to that for years!

That will make a pretty full first day. On our second day, we'll visit bustling Chinatown for a delicious lunch. Then we'll go to the Exploratorium, the huge science and art museum. Later that night, we're going to see a play at the Herbst Theatre. Lastly, on our third day, we plan to visit Alcatraz, the famous island prison in the San Francisco Bay. The whole trip will be a short one, but worth every minute!

Graphic organizers can help you identify chronological order. In this graphic organizer, list five things the narrator plans to do, in the order that she will do them.

1.	2.	3.	4.	5.

DIRECTIONS
Read this biography of a famous American writer and scholar. Use what you have learned about chronological order to answer the questions. Make a graphic organizer on a separate sheet of paper to organize your thoughts.

Zora Neale Hurston: American Folklorist

Zora Neale Hurston was born in 1891 in Notasulga, Alabama. At a young age, she moved to rural Eatonville, Florida—the first all-black town to be incorporated in the United States. At age 13, she lost her mother and had to move from relative to relative. Hurston worked her way through high school holding such jobs as maid and waitress.

After two years at Morgan Academy in Baltimore, Hurston attended Howard University in Washington, D.C. She then moved to New York City to study at Barnard College. There she studied African and African American folklore.

During her time at Barnard, Hurston published several short stories and articles. She graduated Barnard in 1928. She then spent many years doing anthropological research in the rural South. Some of the folklore she collected appeared in her 1935 collection, *Mules and Men*.

Hurston is most famous for her dramatic, poetic novel *Their Eyes Were Watching God* (1937). Deeply rooted in folklore, it is the story of Janie Crawford, a young black woman from Eatonville who searches for love, happiness, and her own voice. With great strength, Janie faces many challenges—even a hurricane and a husband bitten by a rabid dog.

When Hurston died in 1960, she left behind a body of work that captured the spirit and experience of the African American culture of the South like no other writer from the 1920s and 1930s.

1. What did Hurston do right after she attended Howard University?

    HINT: Look for clue words that tell you chronological order.

    _____

2. Which publication mentioned in this passage came out first? What year was it published?

    HINT: Look for dates when identifying chronological order.

    _____

3. List four words from this passage that help you understand the chronological order. Then underline all the phrases in the passage that show specific dates in Hurston's life.

    HINT: Clue words that show sequence and order often appear at the beginning of a sentence.

    _____

Step 3

DIRECTIONS
Read this memo posted on a high school wall. Then answer the questions.

How to Vote

(1) Voting is the most cherished right of citizens of the United States. All U.S. citizens, once they turn 18, have the right to vote for the candidates of their choice on Election Day.

(2) But how does one go about voting?

(3) The first step is to register. You can't vote unless you are registered. Registering is easy: you just need your state's voter registration form. You can find this form online at various Web sites. You might also get the form at your school, post office, or at a local voter registration agency.

(4) Once you get the form, follow the simple directions to complete it. Next, mail the form to the address listed on it, which is your state's election office. (In some states, you need to fill out the form in person at the election office.)

(5) The next step is to find out where to vote. Once you're registered, you'll receive information in the mail about where your polling center is. It might be inside a school or a community center. Keep this mailing handy so you'll know where to go on Election Day.

(6) After you know where to vote, learn about the candidates! It's important to know as much about the candidates as you can. Become an educated voter by reading and watching news about candidates; visiting candidates' Web sites; reading mailings the candidates send you; and talking with friends and family about the candidates and the issues you care about.

(7) The final step is to go to the polls! When Election Day comes, visit your polling center and cast your vote. Make sure your voice is heard!

Circle the letter of the best answer.

1. What does a person need to do before finding out where to vote?

   A. Fill out a voter registration form and mail it.

   B. Learn about the candidates.

   C. Go to the polls and vote.

   D. Find out when Election Day is.

2. What is the next step after acquiring the registration form?

   A. Mail it to the election office.

   B. Follow the directions to complete it.

   C. Find out where to vote.

   D. Learn about the candidates.

3. Which of these is NOT a step required for voting?

   A. going to your polling center

   B. finding out where to vote

   C. registering to vote

   D. campaigning for a candidate

4. Which clue word in paragraph 6 indicates order?

   A. become

   B. important

   C. after

   D. issues

DIRECTIONS

Read this news article about three inventive young men. Use the Reading Guide for tips on analyzing chronological order. Then answer the questions on the next page.

Raiders Remake

1. It was the summer of 1982, and *Raiders of the Lost Ark* was one of the biggest blockbusters around. In fact, three kids in south Mississippi were so excited by the movie, they decided to re-make it, shot-for-shot, playing the main characters themselves.

2. First, 11-year-old Chris Strompolos contacted a classmate, Eric Zala, who had made a small movie for school. Strompolos asked Zala if he would help him re-make *Raiders.* "I just wanted to create that environment myself and be Indiana Jones as a kid," Strompolos told Public Radio International in an interview. "It was a pursuit of a fantasy."

3. After Zala agreed to the project, the boys enlisted another classmate, Jayson Lamb, who knew a lot about special effects.

4. Then they began planning the project. Strompolos would indeed play Indiana Jones, the daring archeologist played by Harrison Ford. Zala would direct the movie and play Dr. Belloq, Jones's arch enemy. Lamb would work the camera and handle special effects.

5. The three friends created a storyboard of all the scenes and began videotaping. They continued taping over summers—for the next seven years! They shot jungle scenes in Strompolos's backyard. They shot cave scenes in Zala's basement. They used plastic skulls and a homemade fiberglass boulder. A neighbor donated an old pick-up truck for a famous chase scene. A group of animal wranglers provided garden snakes for several snake scenes.

6. In 1989, their movie was finally complete. It is called *Raiders of the Lost Ark: The Adaptation.* For years, it mostly stayed on Zala's shelf, and only a few people saw it. Then, in 2003, a copy fell into the hands of a filmmaker who sent it to Steven Spielberg, director of the original *Raiders of the Lost Ark* film.

7. Spielberg then wrote the young filmmakers a letter, congratulating them. "Then it was complete," Strompolos said. "That was the dream." Since then, several audiences have enjoyed the exciting re-make in special screenings. "Still to this day, we all feel [*Raiders* is] just a perfect movie," Strompolos said.

Reading Guide

What is the first thing Chris Strompolos did?

....

Did Jayson Lamb join the project before or after Eric Zala did?

....

What clue word in paragraph 4 helps explain the order of events?

....

How many years after finishing their movie did the filmmakers hear from Steven Spielberg? How can you tell?

....

What words in paragraph 7 give you information about the order of events? Underline these words.

Circle the letter of the best answer.

1. Which of these statements indicates chronological order?

   A. They used plastic skulls and a homemade fiberglass boulder.

   B. "It was a pursuit of a fantasy."

   C. Spielberg mailed the young filmmakers a letter, congratulating them.

   D. Then they began planning the project.

2. What was the next thing that happened after Zala agreed to re-make *Raiders*?

   A. They created a storyboard of all the scenes.

   B. A filmmaker sent the movie to Steven Spielberg.

   C. Jayson Lamb joined the project.

   D. They finished the movie.

3. What phrase in paragraph 5 gives information about the order of events?

   A. *for the next seven years!*

   B. *an old pick-up truck*

   C. *They shot jungle scenes*

   D. *A neighbor donated*

4. When did Steven Spielberg contact the young filmmakers?

   A. in 1982

   B. in 1989

   C. in 2003

   D. in 2007

5. In paragraph 6, which of these phrases does NOT help you understand sequence?

   A. *In 1989*

   B. *It is called*

   C. *For years*

   D. *Then, in 2003*

A Letter From Young Abe

Springfield, April 1, 1838

Dear Madam:

(1) I shall make the subject of this letter the history of much of my life since I last saw you.

(2) In the autumn of 1836, a married lady of my acquaintance, who was a great friend, proposed that she would bring her sister to visit me—upon condition that I would become her brother-in-law. I, of course, accepted the proposal.

(3) Time passed on. In due time, the lady brought her sister to me. Although I had seen her before, she did not look as my imagination had pictured her. In short, I was not at all pleased with her. But what could I do? I had told her sister that I would marry her, for better or for worse. And I make a point to stick to my word. At once I determined to consider her my wife. This done, I began searching for perfections in her which might fairly offset her defects.

(4) Shortly after this, I traveled. While away, I exchanged letters with her. After my return home, I saw nothing to change my opinion of her in any way. She was the same and so was I. I now spent my time between planning how I might get along through life after we would wed, and how I might delay the evil day, which I really dreaded.

(5) After all my suffering upon this deeply interesting subject, here I am, wholly unexpectedly out of the "scrape." After I had delayed the matter as long as I could—which, by the way, had brought me to last fall—I concluded I should not delay further. And so I made the proposal to her direct. But, shocking to relate, she answered, "No."

(6) I asked again and found she repelled my proposal with greater firmness than before. I tried it again and again, but with the same success, or rather with the same lack of success. I finally was forced to give up, and I very unexpectedly found myself mortified, almost beyond endurance. I then, for the first time, began to suspect that I was really a little in love with her.

(7) But I let it all go. Others have been made fools of by the girls, but this can never be said of me. I most emphatically, in this instance, made a fool of myself. I have now concluded that I will never again think of marrying, for this reason: I can never be satisfied with anyone who would be blockheaded enough to have me.

Your sincere friend,
A. Lincoln

Circle the letter of the best answer.

1. Which of these events happened first, beginning in autumn, 1836?

   A. Lincoln traveled.

   B. A friend brought her sister to visit Lincoln.

   C. A friend proposed bringing her sister to visit Lincoln.

   D. Lincoln was forced to give up repeating his proposal.

2. Which of these phrases does NOT indicate chronological order?

   A. *I then, for the first time*

   B. *After all my suffering*

   C. *In due time*

   D. *I had told her sister*

3. What happened before Lincoln returned home from traveling?

   A. He exchanged letters with his friend's sister.

   B. He proposed to his friend's sister.

   C. He was turned down by his friend's sister.

   D. He concluded he would never think about marrying again.

4. Which clue word in paragraph 4 appears more than once and indicates chronological order?

   A. *her*

   B. *after*

   C. *how*

   D. *might*

5. When did Lincoln conclude he should NOT delay his proposal further?

   A. in the fall of 1837

   B. in the fall of 1836

   C. in April of 1838

   D. It cannot be determined from this letter.

6. What happened after Lincoln proposed to his friend's sister?

   A. She accepted Lincoln's proposal.

   B. She answered, "No."

   C. Lincoln returned home.

   D. Lincoln found himself mortified.

7. What does Lincoln say he was forced to do in the end?

   A. He was forced to marry someone else.

   B. He was forced to propose.

   C. He was forced to write letters.

   D. He was forced to give up.

8. On a separate sheet of paper, create a timeline. Write on the timeline at least five things that happened, as Lincoln describes in his letter. Put these events in the order in which they happened.

Lesson 6 • Compare and Contrast

To **compare** means to find the similarities between two or more things.

To **contrast** means to find the differences between two or more things.

> Both CD players and MP3 players allow a person to listen to music. A CD player needs a disc to play music. An MP3 player keeps the music in its memory.

- Comparison: CD players and MP3 players both play music.
- Contrast: CD players need discs. MP3 players do not.

Example

Read this passage about skiing and snowboarding. Then answer the questions.

Skis or Snowboards

Eric and Donna both enjoy winter sports. They both like to cruise down the side of a snowy mountain. Eric prefers to do it on skis, while Donna would rather ride a snowboard. Eric likes skis because they move faster than a snowboard. Donna would rather do fancy tricks that can't be done on skis. Either way, they both end up having a good time.

Circle the letter of the best answer.

1. How are skis and snowboards similar?

    A. They are both used in the summer.

    B. They are both used on snow.

    C. They are equally fast.

    D. They are both Eric's favorite.

2. What is one way that skis and snowboards are different?

    A. Skis are used by older people.

    B. Snowboards are heavier.

    C. Skis are more expensive.

    D. Skis move faster.

DIRECTIONS
Read this passage about expected ends. Use the Reading Guide for tips. The tips can help you access prior knowledge and find comparisons and contrasts. Then answer the questions on the next page.

adapted and excerpted from

Ethics (350 B.C.E.)

by Aristotle

① Every art and science, every action and choice, aims at some good. ② For this reason, a common description of good is, "that which all things aim at."

③ There is clearly a difference in the end result of these different actions. ④ In some cases, they are acts of working. ⑤ In other cases, there are concrete results beyond the act of working. ⑥ When the end result is more than the act of working, their nature is better.

⑦ Since there are many actions, arts, and sciences, the end results are different. ⑧ In the healing art, for instance, health is the end result. ⑨ In the shipbuilding art, a boat is the end result. ⑩ In the military art, victory.

⑪ Some actions, arts, or sciences have a range of smaller parts. ⑫ For example, the art of horsemanship includes the art of making saddles, the art of horse grooming, and many others. ⑬ In all such cases, the ends of the master-arts are more important than those of the sub-arts because the ends of these sub-arts are only found in order to reach the ends of the master-arts.

Reading Guide

What is Aristotle comparing in sentence 1?

....

What is Aristotle contrasting in sentences 4 and 5?

....

What does Aristotle say is true of all actions, art, and sciences with a range of smaller parts?

Circle the letter of the best answer.

1. What does Aristotle say arts, sciences, actions, and choices have in common?

   A. They aim at some good.

   B. They aim at some evil.

   C. They are all boring.

   D. They are taught in school.

2. According to Aristotle, which is an end that is NOT a concrete result?

   A. joy

   B. friendship

   C. working

   D. peace

3. According to Aristotle, what is one difference between a doctor and a shipbuilder?

   A. The doctor provides boats, and the shipbuilder provides health.

   B. The doctor provides health, and the shipbuilder provides boats.

   C. The doctor provides war, and the shipbuilder provides wood.

   D. The doctor provides truth, and the shipbuilder provides wealth.

4. Which does Aristotle say is MOST important?

   A. a groomed horse

   B. the end of a master-art

   C. a saddle

   D. the end of a sub-art

Step 2

You have learned that to compare means to find similarities and to contrast means to find differences. Here are some comparison and contrast clue words and phrases:

Compare and Contrast Chart	
Compare	**Contrast**
like, likewise	unlike
same as	different from/than
similarly	by contrast, conversely, instead
too, also, as well as, and	but, not, whereas, however
both	as opposed to
in the same manner	on the other hand

Example

Read the following passage about hybrid and electric cars. Look for comparisons and contrasts.

Hybrid and Electric

The future of cars is electricity. Both gas/electric hybrid cars and pure electric cars use it. While both kinds of car cut down on the need for gas, only the electric car uses no gas at all. The hybrid still uses some gas. Both cars have a battery that needs to be recharged. The hybrid battery gets recharged while it uses gas. By contrast, the electric car needs to be plugged in at times. In general, a good thing about hybrids is that they can go faster than electric cars. Then again, using a pure electric car and never having to buy gas again is pretty good, too.

Fill in the diagram below to show your understanding of comparisons and contrasts. Write the hybrid's unique characteristics in the left oval. Write the electric car's unique characteristics in the right oval. Write characteristics they share in the overlap.

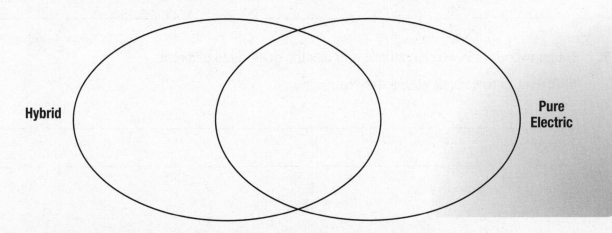

DIRECTIONS
Read this passage about guitars. Then use what you have learned to find comparisons and contrasts to answer the questions. Make a graphic organizer on a separate sheet of paper to organize your thoughts.

Guitars

A guitar is a stringed instrument that is used in many styles of music. In general, there are two types of guitar: acoustic and electric. An acoustic guitar can be played anywhere, on its own. An electric guitar, however, needs a power source. Both types of guitar use vibrations to produce sound. They are also similar in that they have strings of different thicknesses to produces different notes. The acoustic guitar is a simpler instrument. When a string is struck, it vibrates. These vibrations echo inside the hollow wooden body of the guitar and sound is produced. The electric guitar, on the other hand, usually does not have a hollow body where vibrations can echo. Instead, there are devices called pickups attached to the guitar under the strings. Pickups are basically magnets that capture the vibrations of the strings and change them into an electric signal. The signal then travels down a wire to an electric speaker that produces the sound.

1.   List four comparison and contrast clue words or phrases that you find in the passage.

   HINT: Use the clue word and phrase list on the previous page.

_____

_____

2.   Name two ways in which acoustic and electric guitars are similar.

   HINT: Look for comparison clue words and phrases.

_____

_____

3.   Name two ways in which acoustic and electric guitars are different.

   HINT: Look for contrast clue words and phrases.

_____

_____

Step 3

DIRECTIONS
Read this passage about Earth and the human body. Then answer the questions.

adapted and excerpted from

The Treatise on Water (1509)

by Leonardo da Vinci

The ancients have called the human body the world in miniature. This name is well given because the human body is very like Earth. As the human body has bones to support its flesh, the world has rocks to support it. The human body has lungs that rise and fall in breathing. Likewise, Earth has ocean tides that rise and fall as if the world itself breathes. Blood flows through veins that run throughout the human body. Similarly, water travels through springs all across Earth.

Earth lacks sinews and muscle because these are simply for movement. Since Earth does not move the way the human body does, muscles are not needed. In all other points, however, they are very much alike.

Circle the letter of the best answer.

1. Why has the human body been called "the world in miniature"?

   A. The world is shrinking.

   B. The human body is not like Earth.

   C. The human body is very like Earth.

   D. The human body is made of rocks.

2. According to da Vinci, rocks are similar to the human body's

   A. veins.

   B. bones.

   C. flesh.

   D. muscles.

3. According to da Vinci, what makes the Earth seem to breathe?

   A. the rise and fall of its tides

   B. the rise and fall of its lungs

   C. the different directions of its winds

   D. the push and pull of its muscles

4. What does da Vinci say makes the world different from the human body?

   A. Earth has no veins.

   B. Earth has no blood.

   C. Earth has no bones.

   D. Earth has no muscles.

DIRECTIONS
Read the passage. Use the Reading Guide for tips that can help you compare and contrast.
Then answer the questions on the next page.

At Odds

Neil looked horrified as a juicy meatball rolled toward him across the table, leaving a trail of marinara in its wake. "Must you eat like that?" he said.

"Like what?" Leon answered, as pasta tumbled out of his mouth onto his shirt. He pulled the pasta from his badly stained T-shirt and stuffed it back into his full mouth.

Neil glanced down at his own immaculate button-down shirt and delicately picked off a piece of lint. He ironed his shirts daily, and it showed.

Leon picked up another meatball with his fingers. Neil could not believe his eyes. He held up his fork.

"Do you recognize this device?" he asked.

"No," said Leon. "What is it?"

"Hilarious."

"Why, thank you."

Neil cringed as he watched Leon run his filthy hand through his greasy shoulder-length gray hair, then pick up more spaghetti with his fingers. Neil prided himself on his short blonde hair, which he had trimmed every two weeks.

When Leon stood up from the table, a shower of bread crumbs fell to the floor. Reaching immediately for the broom, Neil watched Leon shuffle past the orderly and spotless bedroom and enter his own pigsty.

When Leon came back out, slumped onto the couch, and turned on the television, Neil headed for the front door. He hated television, especially the reality shows Frank watched.

Reading Guide

What does the second paragraph tell you about how Neil is different from Leon?

....

Do the two characters dress the same way?

....

Does Neil agree with the way Leon looks?

....

Who sleeps in the orderly bedroom?

....

Which difference between the two characters causes Neil to leave?

Circle the letter of the best answer.

1. What are Neil's table manners like?

   A. He has bad table manners.

   B. He has good table manners.

   C. He eats with his hands.

   D. He never eats.

2. How are Leon's clothes different from Neil's?

   A. Leon cares about his appearance.

   B. Neil does not care about his appearance.

   C. Leon does not care about his appearance.

   D. Leon wears only blue clothing.

3. What is the difference between the two characters' hair styles?

   A. Leon has long greasy hair. Neil has short neat hair.

   B. Leon has short greasy hair. Neil has long neat hair.

   C. Leon has long neat hair. Neil has short greasy hair.

   D. Leon has short neat hair. Neil has long greasy hair.

4. What do the two bedrooms tell you about the two characters?

   A. Both characters are messy.

   B. Leon is neat, and Neil is a slob.

   C. Both characters are neat.

   D. Neil is neat, and Leon is a slob.

5. Do the two characters enjoy the same forms of entertainment?

   A. Only Leon likes television.

   B. Only Neil likes television.

   C. They both like television.

   D. They both hate television.

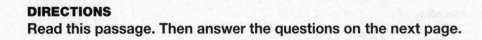

DIRECTIONS
Read this passage. Then answer the questions on the next page.

Pop Goes the Soda

by Alexandra Lapiz

It is interesting that people from different backgrounds or parts of the country call the same items by different names. For example, there are many names for a carbonated beverage. Many people call it *soda*. Others call it *pop*. Another common name is *soft drink*. There are even people who call any carbonated drink a *tonic*.

A sandwich with various ingredients on a long bun has many names as well. It can be called a *hero*, a *hoagie*, a *submarine*, a *grinder*, or a *poor boy*. What people call this sandwich depends on where they are from.

Some people call shoes used for athletics *sneakers*. Many call them *tennis shoes*. Still others call them *gym shoes*.

What do you call the insects that fly around and light up? There are people who call them *fireflies*. There are also people who call them *lightning bugs*.

If you have a drink made of milk and ice cream, would you call it a *milkshake* or a *frappe*? If you have small bits of candy on top of your ice cream, what would you call those? Many people call them *sprinkles*. Others refer to them as *jimmies*.

If you wanted water from your kitchen sink, would you get it from the *faucet,* the *spigot*, or the *tap*? The answer depends on where you grew up.

Many people enjoy eating chicken wings with a spicy sauce. Some people believe this dish was invented in Buffalo, New York, so they call them *Buffalo wings*. Other people just call them *hot wings*.

If your mom wanted you to get something from the area of your house that is below the ground, would she tell you to go to the *basement* or the *cellar?*

You may not have even heard of some of these names people use for things. This does not mean they are wrong. One name for something is not better than another. People from different areas simply call things by different names.

86

Circle the letter of the best answer.

1. Which item has the MOST names listed in the passage?

   A. carbonated beverage

   B. long sandwich

   C. athletic shoe

   D. spicy chicken wing

2. What determines what people call a long sandwich?

   A. how old they are

   B. how tall they are

   C. where they are from

   D. what is on the sandwich

3. Which is NOT a name for *athletic shoes*?

   A. dancing shoes

   B. sneakers

   C. gym shoes

   D. tennis shoes

4. If you wanted a milkshake with sprinkles on top, what else could you say?

   A. an egg cream with frillies

   B. a tonic with sprinkles

   C. a milkshake with shingles

   D. a frappe with jimmies

5. According to the passage, where does water come from?

   A. a well

   B. an ocean

   C. a spigot

   D. a lake

6. Why do some people call spicy chicken wings *Buffalo wings*?

   A. The dish was invented in Buffalo.

   B. The people are from Buffalo.

   C. They are actually made from buffalos.

   D. They like the word *buffalo*.

7. What is another word for *basement*?

   A. dirt box

   B. sub-kitchen

   C. cellar

   D. upstairs

8. On a separate sheet of paper, give another example of an item with more than one name, or think of another name used for any item in the passage.

Lesson 7 • Cause and Effect

A **cause** is a reason why something happens. An **effect** is the result of a cause.

Cause	Effect
Magdalena drove through a stop sign.	Magdalena received a traffic ticket.
Justine ate extra spicy chilly.	Justine drank a lot of water.
Max got home five hours after curfew.	Max's parents grounded him for a week.

Example

Read this passage and identify the causes and effects. Then answer the questions.

I woke up late and missed the bus. This stinks. I've been late twice already this month, and you get after-school detention on your third tardy. Detention lasts an hour, so that means I won't get out until 3:30 today. That also means I'm going to miss my piano lesson! That's the worst part of all. I've got my piano recital tomorrow and really need today's lesson. All of this is because I woke up late.

Circle the letter of the best answer.

1. What is the cause of the narrator getting detention?

   A. She missed the bus.

   B. This is her third tardy in a month.

   C. She woke up late.

   D. She has to stay at school until 3:30.

2. What is the effect of the narrator getting detention?

   A. She is going to leave school early.

   B. She is going to miss her piano lesson.

   C. She is going to miss her piano recital.

   D. She is going to wake up.

DIRECTIONS
Read this story and answer the questions that follow. Use the Reading Guide to help you identify cause and effect. Then answer the questions on the next page.

Peak Oil Theory

(1) The world runs on oil. (2) Oil powers the cars, trucks, boats and airplanes that transport people and trade goods all over the world. (3) It fuels industry and heats our homes.

(4) Oil is a nonrenewable resource. (5) That means that it can't be recycled. (6) When oil is burned to power an engine, it is gone forever. (7) Since the industrial revolution, the world has depended on oil to power a lot of engines. (8) Oil is like food for industry. (9) If there is no oil, industry will starve. (10) If industry starves, factories will close and people will lose their jobs. (11) If people lose their jobs, they can't afford to own homes or buy food. (12) If we ever truly run out of oil, it will completely change the way we live their our lives.

(13) Some people think oil production is nearing or past its peak. (14) They say there is not enough oil left to meet the world's demand for it. (15) If the supply of oil decreases while the demand for it increases, the price of oil will increase. (16) This seems to be playing out right now. (17) Oil prices are at all-time highs.

(18) The most obvious impact comes at gas station pumps. (19) The price for a gallon of gas has tripled since the 1990s. (20) A person driving a gas-guzzling sport utility vehicle who paid $30 to fill his tank five years ago is paying close to $100 now.

(21) The problem with the depleting oil supply goes a lot further. (22) Rising energy costs will be felt everywhere. (23) Most things we buy in stores are transported from other locations. (24) Sometimes they are shipped on boats from overseas. (25) Other times, they are transported in tractor trailers from other parts of the country. (26) Oil price increases will lead to higher shipping costs, and higher shipping costs will lead to higher prices at grocery stores, department stores, and everywhere goods are sold.

(27) If the world is really running out of oil, people will have to depend on local resources to avoid paying painful prices for shipped goods and look for alternate methods of transportation.

Reading Guide

What is the overall reason the world is running out of oil?

....

Why is oil more expensive than it used to be?

....

What are some impacts of rising energy costs?

....

What will happen if the world runs out of oil?

Circle the letter of the best answer.

1. What happens when oil is burned to power an engine?

    A. The engine breaks down.

    B. The oil is gone forever.

    C. The price of oil increases

    D. The oil supply increases.

2. What could people losing their jobs lead to?

    A. Workers will not be able to afford gas to get to work.

    B. Workers will go on strike.

    C. Factories will close.

    D. Industry will not be able to afford to pay workers.

3. Why is oil more expensive than it used to be?

    A. There is more supply.

    B. There is less demand.

    C. There is more demand and less supply.

    D. There is less demand and more supply.

4. What will happen if the world runs out of oil?

    A. Industry will expand.

    B. The demand for solar energy will decrease.

    C. People will depend on local resources.

    D. People will import more resources.

You have learned that a cause is a reason why something happens and an effect is the result of a cause. You can recognize cause-and-effect relationships by looking for cue words and phrases like *due to, because, since, so, as a result,* and *as a result of.*

One cause can have many effects.

> As class president, Becca, will have to come in early every morning, stay late every day, and organize several events.

Writers sometimes show the effect before the cause.

> The *Titanic* sank because it struck an iceberg.

Example

Read the following passage. Try to focus on the cause-and-effect relationships.

Charlie Mingus

Charlie Mingus was born in 1922 and died 56 years later of Lou Gehrig's disease. Mingus was dedicated to his instrument and is recognized as a major 20th century composer and one of the best bass players in the history of jazz. He is known as much for his personality as his playing because he had a temper that earned him the nickname "The Angry Man of Jazz." Musicians lucky enough to play with him said his desire to perform and the unusual things he did on stage came from his need to relieve stress.

Now fill in the chart below to show your understanding of cause and effect. Write down causes in the left column and effects in the right column.

Cause	Effect

DIRECTIONS
Read this story about alien hand syndrome. Use what you have learned about cause and effect to answer the questions. Make a graphic organizer on a separate sheet of paper to organize your thoughts.

An Unusual Syndrome

Some years back, I was in a motorcycle accident. I ran a stop sign and hit a car. I went flying fifty yards through the air, hit the ground, and slid another fifteen yards. I woke up ten years after the accident because I had been in a coma. Pretty hard to imagine—it's like going to sleep one night and waking up ten years later.

That's not even the worst of it. It wasn't until after I came out of the coma that the really weird stuff started to happen. I lay in my bed at the hospital watching television one night when the channel started to change by itself. I looked around to see who was doing this and realized it was me. I had the remote control in my hand, but there was no sensation. My hand was changing the channels by itself. It's like my hand was acting on its own.

Needless to say this frightened me. I screamed for the nurse. I told her what was happening, and she told me to calm down and the doctor would be by to see me.

Long story short: they ran all sorts of tests on me and concluded I had something called Alien Hand Syndrome. You probably think I'm joking, but no. It's a real condition. Research it if you don't believe me. The doctor said it was because I'd been in a coma for so long, the communication lines between my brain and my hand got rusty. So now I've got no control over my left hand. Makes for some unusual situations.

1. Why did the author go into a coma?

   HINT: A cause happens before an effect.

   _____

2. How did the author get Alien Hand Syndrome?

   HINT: What caused this unique problem?

   _____

3. List some possible effects of alien hand syndrome that the author hints at in the last paragraph.

   HINT: The author says that the syndrome makes for some unusual moments.

   _____

DIRECTIONS
Read this passage about the movement of plants. Then answer the questions.

adapted and excerpted from

The Power of Movement in Plants (1880)

by Charles Darwin

This book will show that every growing part of every growing plant is always turning in a circular path. Often, this is on a very small scale. Even the underground stems and roots of seedlings turn. Of course, these can only turn as much as the dirt around them will allow.

This circular turning is the basic movement that lets every plant move in more complex ways. Sweeping movements made by plant stems and vines are really just larger versions of this turning motion. It is this turning motion in one direction that causes the blades and leaves of a plant to find their places. At night, the leaves of many plants take an upright position to protect themselves from the cold air. Once again, this upright turning of the leaves is the result of the same circular movement.

Circle the letter of the best answer.

1. Why is the movement of plant roots limited?

   A. They are lazy.

   B. They are too slow.

   C. They are held by dirt.

   D. They refuse to turn.

2. What is one effect of the turning motion in plants?

   A. Plants look like they are dancing.

   B. Plants are able to make complicated movements.

   C. Plants twist themselves back into the ground.

   D. Plants tie themselves into knots.

3. How do plant leaves find their positions?

   A. They turn in a constant direction.

   B. They fight each other for a spot.

   C. Gravity holds them in the right places.

   D. They each have a very small brain.

4. Why do plant leaves turn upright at night?

   A. They are shy in the dark.

   B. The air is colder at night.

   C. They think it looks better.

   D. There is no gravity at night.

DIRECTIONS
Read the story. Use the Reading Guide for tips that can help you determine cause and effect as you read. Then answer the questions on the next page.

adapted and excerpted from

Beowulf (circa 1000)

by Anonymous

The hated monster Grendel came across the land in search of men to eat. He walked until he came to the reinforced door of the king's palace. With a mighty blow, full of rage, he burst the door from its hinges. Then he crossed the floor of the palace hall, his eyes flashing like fire.

Grendel came to a room full of sleeping men. There he was filled with the urge to kill and feed on all of these men. Although he did not know it, fate would not allow him to ever seize another man after this night. This was because of the hero Beowulf, who was secretly watching him. Beowulf was silently sizing up his enemy for their upcoming battle. As Beowulf looked on, Grendel picked up a sleeping man, tore him apart, drank the blood in streams, and ate the body piece by piece.

Then, continuing across the room, Grendel reached his wicked claw toward the hero Beowulf. Beowulf grabbed the monster's claw and held it fast. When Grendel realized that the hero's grip was as strong as his own, he tried to flee. Beowulf did not let go and was dragged into the great palace hall. Their raging battle continued and the noise of it woke the other people in the palace.

As the people gathered to watch, they were surprised that the palace could stand up to the extreme crashing violence of the battle. The palace's strength was due to many iron bands built into and around it. The noise continued to increase. Every person standing by was filled with fear by the horrible pained wailing of the monster as Beowulf held him in his mighty grip.

Reading Guide

Why was the monster hated?

Who will cause the monster to never eat anyone after this night?

Why did the monster try to flee?

How did the palace stand up to the battle?

What frightened the onlookers?

Circle the letter of the best answer.

1. Why does the monster come to the palace?

   A. to get exercise

   B. to find friends

   C. to eat people

   D. to fix the door

2. Why does Beowulf watch Grendel?

   A. to gauge his strength

   B. to watch him eat

   C. to cure his own boredom

   D. to make a new friend

3. Why is Beowulf dragged into the hall?

   A. He is playing a game with the monster.

   B. The monster cannot shake his grip.

   C. He has tied himself to the monster.

   D. The monster will not let go of him.

4. Which phrase in the last paragraph gives a clue to the reason the palace is so strong?

   A. as the

   B. of the

   C. due to

   D. by the

5. Why does the monster wail?

   A. He is a baby.

   B. The people hate him.

   C. The palace fell on him.

   D. Beowulf's grip is painful.

DIRECTIONS
Read this essay about a civic duty. Then answer the questions on the next page.

adapted and excerpted from

On the Duty of Civil Disobedience (1849)

by Henry David Thoreau

Unlike those who wish for no government, I ask for better government. If every person would say what kind of government would earn his or her respect, we would be one step closer to having it.

The true reason why, when power is in the hands of the people, a majority is allowed to rule is not because it is most likely to be right, not because this is fairest to the minority, but because it is physically stronger. A government in which the majority always rules cannot be based on fairness. Can't there be a government in which conscience decides right and wrong, and the majority decides only practical questions? Must the citizen let the lawmaker act as his or her conscience? If so, then why does each person have a conscience? I think we should be people first and citizens afterward. People should respect what is right, not just the law. The only duty I have is to do what I think is right. A group itself has no conscience, but a group of thoughtful people is a group with a conscience.

Laws never made people more fair. Respect for unfair laws turns even the most well-meaning people into tools of unfairness. A common and natural result of thoughtless respect for the law is seen in a group of soldiers marching off to war against their wills, against their common sense, and against their consciences. This makes the marching very hard and causes the heart to skip a beat. These soldiers are peaceful people deep down. They know they are getting involved in some awful business. So, are they people at all, or are they just tools in the hands of dishonest politicians?

Circle the letter of the best answer.

1. What is the effect of people stating what kind of government they want?

   A. They would sound foolish to lawmakers.

   B. The present government would fall.

   C. They would be closer to getting it.

   D. They would lose their right to vote.

2. Why is the majority allowed to rule?

   A. It is smarter.

   B. It is always right.

   C. It is more fair.

   D. It is stronger.

3. Why does Thoreau ask why people have consciences?

   A. He thinks people make stupid decisions.

   B. He thinks people do not think for themselves.

   C. He thinks people are cruel to each other.

   D. He thinks people are dishonest.

4. What is the result of a group of thoughtful people?

   A. a group with a conscience

   B. a group with no conscience

   C. a fair form of government

   D. a group of soldiers

5. What happens when people respect unfair laws?

   A. Those people become smarter.

   B. Those people become fairer.

   C. Those people become unfair.

   D. Those people become soldiers.

6. Which phrase tells the reader that what happens when one has a "thoughtless respect for the law" will be revealed?

   A. even the most

   B. is seen in

   C. are they just

   D. result of

7. What are two effects of soldiers marching against their wills?

   A. They refuse to fight, and they are punished.

   B. The march seems difficult, and their hearts skip beats.

   C. They stop marching, and they change sides.

   D. Their hearts skip beats, and they become politicians.

8. On a separate sheet of paper, describe another possible "common and natural result of thoughtless respect for the law."

Lesson 8 • Fact and Opinion

A **fact** is a statement that can be verified in a reference source such as an encyclopedia, a dictionary, a map, or a history book. The statement "Key lime pie is a dessert made from the juice of key limes" is a fact because it can be verified.

An **opinion** is a statement that shows a personal belief or viewpoint. Statements that express that something is good or bad in some way are usually opinions. The statement "Key lime pie is the yummiest dessert on the whole planet" is an opinion. It expresses a belief that this dessert is good.

Example

Read this excerpt from a report on Benjamin Franklin. Then answer the questions.

A Very Smart Man

Of all our Founding Fathers, Benjamin Franklin was the smartest. In addition to being an influential politician, Franklin was also a writer, a printer, a scientist, and a musician. He was even Postmaster General at one point. Franklin was America's greatest inventor ever. His many inventions include bifocals and the lightning rod. We would have never known about electricity without him. We might not have not have gained our independence either.

Circle the letter of the best answer.

1. Which of these statements is a fact?

   A. Of all our Founding Fathers, Benjamin Franklin was the smartest.

   B. Franklin was America's greatest inventor ever.

   C. He was even Postmaster General at one point.

   D. We might not have gained our independence either.

2. "We would have never known about electricity without him" is an opinion because

   A. it can be verified.

   B. it states a personal belief.

   C. it is in the encyclopedia.

   D. nobody would believe this.

DIRECTIONS
Read this student's persuasive essay on driver's licenses. Use the Reading Guide to help you distinguish between fact and opinion. Then answer the questions on the next page.

Keep Teen Drivers Safe

(1) A debate is underway in our great state that will affect every teenager in it. The question is whether our state needs tougher driver's license restrictions for teen drivers. The answer, of course, is yes.

(2) Currently, we do not have a "graduated driver's license" law. Such a law would give teens certain freedoms on the road *only* as they gain more experience. Most states do have laws like this. It's time we join them and embrace this great idea.

(3) A graduated license usually has three stages. The first stage is getting a learner's permit. Drivers with learner's permits have to drive a certain amount of time with a licensed driver. The second stage is an intermediate license. This license lets teens drive unsupervised, but with certain restrictions. The restrictions might include not driving at certain hours of night or with young passengers. The last stage is a full driver's license.

(4) We all know that teens take risks—sometimes far too many. This applies when we're behind the wheel, too. Who's going to stop us from goofing off when we're driving alone or out cruising with our friends? Who doesn't like showing off a little and putting the petal to the metal?

(5) But there's a deadly cost to our risk-taking. The AAA Foundation for Traffic Safety says that car crashes are the leading cause of death among teens. According to one recent study, about a third of the people killed in accidents involving 15-, 16-, and 17-year-old drivers are the teen drivers themselves.

(6) We cannot afford to lose our young people to loose licensing rules. I believe our state should adopt a strict three-stage licensing program. And we need to do this before it's too late. The lives of our young people are at stake. The citizens of this state must stand up and act right now.

Reading Guide

Look for statements throughout this essay that can be verified. Those statements are facts.

Does paragraph 2 contain all facts, all opinions, or both facts and opinions? How can you tell?

Look for words throughout the essay that show what the author thinks or believes. These signal opinions.

Circle four facts in this essay. Underline four opinions.

Circle the letter of the best answer.

1. Which statement from the essay is a fact?

    A. And we need to do this before it's too late.

    B. The AAA Foundation for Traffic Safety says that car crashes are the leading cause of death among teens.

    C. The citizens of this state must stand up and act now.

    D. The answer, of course, is yes.

2. Which statement in paragraph 2 is an opinion?

    A. Currently, we do not have a "graduated driver's license" law.

    B. Such a law would give teens certain freedoms on the road *only* as they gain more experience.

    C. Most states do have laws like this.

    D. It's time we join them and embrace this great idea.

3. In paragraph 3, the statement "The first stage is getting a learner's permit" is a fact because

    A. it makes a lot of sense.

    B. everyone knows it is true.

    C. it can be looked up and verified.

    D. it shows a personal belief.

4. How can you tell if a statement is a fact or an opinion?

    A. Opinions can be verified, whereas facts cannot.

    B. Facts can be verified, whereas opinions cannot.

    C. Both facts and opinions can be verified, so there is no difference between them.

    D. There is no way to tell if a statement is a fact or an opinion.

Step 2

It is important to tell the difference between facts and opinions when evaluating texts. You have learned that a fact can be verified in reference sources whereas an opinion cannot be.

Another way to tell if something is not a fact, but an opinion, is to look for key words that express personal feelings or beliefs, such as *think* and *believe.* Words that make comparisons or judgments, such as *beautiful, horrible,* and *best,* also signify opinions. Study these opinion words:

Opinion Words	
Personal feeling words	*think, believe, suggest, perhaps, probably, usually, typically, should, must*
Judgment words	*good, bad, best, worst, most, least, always, never, all, none, fantastic, terrible, amazing, awful*

Example

Now read the following passage. Look for facts and opinions.

The Hindenburg

It was the worst disaster in aviation history. Ninety-seven people were bound to the United States from Frankfurt, Germany, aboard the German zeppelin LZ 129 *Hindenburg.* They arrived at their destination of Lakehurst, New Jersey, on May 6, 1937. At 7:25 P.M., while the 804-foot aircraft was landing, the rear of the ship caught fire and burst into flames. People on the ground watched helplessly as thirty-six people perished in a fiery ball that came crashing to the ground.

The zeppelin's makers had used hydrogen, which is flammable, as the lift gas instead of helium, which is not flammable. They never should have flown the aircraft using hydrogen. The *Hindenburg* disaster marked the saddest day in all of the 1930s.

Graphic organizers can help you distinguish fact from opinion. In this graphic organizer, list facts and opinions from this passage. Then underline all words that indicate an opinion.

Facts	Opinions

DIRECTIONS

Read this newspaper article about a recent space mission. Use what you have learned about fact and opinion to answer the questions. Make a graphic organizer on a separate sheet of paper to organize your thoughts.

A New Look at Mercury

A NASA spacecraft recently took surprising new photos of the planet Mercury. One image, taken by the space probe *Messenger*, resembles a giant spider in the middle of a huge crater, NASA scientists said.

The spider image is "unlike anything we've seen anywhere in the solar system," mission chief scientist Sean Solomon of the Carnegie Institution of Washington told the Associated Press (AP).

The closest planet to the sun, Mercury is often considered similar to Earth's moon. But the new images show some differences, such as areas of red and blue. "Mercury doesn't look like the moon," scientist Louise Prockter of Johns Hopkins University, which runs the *Messenger* mission for NASA, told the AP.

Robert Strom, a retired planetary scientist who was part of the *Messenger* team, had a strong reaction to the new photos. "What I saw was astounding to me," Strom told the AP. Strom had earlier worked on the *Mariner 10* spacecraft, which photographed Mercury in 1974 and 1975. "This is a whole new planet we're looking at," Strom said.

The *Messenger* probe took 1,213 photos of Mercury. It is expected to fly by the planet again in the future and take additional pictures.

1. How does planetary scientist Robert Strom feel about the new images of Mercury?

   HINT: You can read his exact words inside quotation marks.

   _____

2. List two statements from this article that are facts.

   HINT: A fact is a statement that can be looked up and verified.

   _____

3. List two opinions from this article. List at least two words that signify opinions.

   HINT: In newspaper articles, these are almost always found inside quotation marks.

   _____

   _____

Step 3

DIRECTIONS
Read this shampoo advertisement from a magazine. Then answer the questions.

Tame Your Hair With Tamezol!

(1) Does your hair have a bad attitude? Have you had enough trying to tame that frizzy, dry, messy mane that just won't do what you tell it?

(2) Well, say goodbye to bad-behaving hair forever. Tamezol shampoo's unique new formula turns unmanageable hair into hair that obeys. Tamezol's ingredients include lemon peel extract, orange fruit juice, potato starch, and eucalyptus leaf. These give your hair that slick, stylish sophistication you've been searching for.

(3) Use just a small dab of Tamezol and feel its moisturizing agents working at once. When you rinse, your hair will feel its silkiest, smoothest, shiniest, and sleekest. It will be soft to the touch and dazzling to the eye.

(4) Tamezol comes in six luscious fragrances: Citrus Garden; Raspberry Bouquet; Caramel Chai Latte; Grapefruit Smoothie; Apple Strudel Delight; and Wild About Walnuts.

(5) It's sold in drug stores, grocery stores, and other retail outlets. Look for the florescent orange bottle wherever fine hair-care products are shelved. Try Tamezol once, and your hair will never misbehave again!

Circle the letter of the best answer.

1. Which statement is a fact?

    A. It will be soft to the touch and dazzling to the eye.

    B. Tamezol's ingredients include lemon peel extract, fruit juice, potato starch, and eucalyptus leaf.

    C. Well, say goodbye to bad-behaving hair forever.

    D. Does your hair have a bad attitude?

2. One opinion about Tamezol is that

    A. it comes in a florescent orange bottle.

    B. it is sold in drug stores, grocery stores, and other retail outlets.

    C. it comes in six fragrances.

    D. if you try it once, your hair will never misbehave again.

3. The adjectives *silkiest, smoothest, shiniest,* and *sleekest* in paragraph 3 signal opinions because they

    A. make comparisons and judgments.

    B. can be believed by everybody.

    C. can be checked in a reference source.

    D. can be proven true or false.

4. Which word in paragraph 5 indicates an opinion?

    A. sold

    B. never

    C. wherever

    D. misbehave

DIRECTIONS
Read this speech by French physicist, chemist, and Nobel laureate Marie Curie. Use the Reading Guide for tips to distinguish fact from opinion. Then answer the questions on the next page.

adapted and excerpted from

"On the Discovery of Uranium" (1921)

by Marie Curie

(1) I could tell you many things about radium and radioactivity. But I shall only give you a short account of my early work. Radium is no more a baby. It is more than 20 years old. But the conditions of the discovery were somewhat peculiar. So it is always of interest to remember them and explain them.

(2) In 1897, I was working on uranium rays, which had been discovered two years before. I thought there should be some unknown element having a much greater radioactivity than uranium. I wanted to find and separate that element. It took many years of hard work.

(3) The special interest of radium is in the intensity of its rays. They are several million times greater than uranium rays. The most important property of the rays is the production of physiological effects on human cells. These effects may be used to cure several diseases. Particularly important is the treatment of cancer.

(4) For medical use, it is necessary to get the element in sufficient quantities. America produces many grams of radium every year. But the price is still very high. The radium is more than a hundred thousand times dearer than gold.

(5) We must not forget that when radium was discovered, no one knew that it would prove useful in hospitals. The work was one of pure science. Scientific work must not be considered from the point of view of its direct usefulness. It must be done for itself, for the beauty of science. Then there is always the chance a scientific discovery will also benefit humanity.

(6) The scientific history of radium is beautiful. The properties of the rays have been studied very closely. We know that particles are expelled from radium with a very great velocity near to that of light. We know that the atoms of radium are destroyed by expulsion of these particles. We know that radioactive elements are constantly disintegrating, and they produce at the end ordinary elements, principally helium and lead.

(7) There is always a vast field of experimentation remaining. Some of you should carry on this scientific work and make a permanent contribution to science.

Reading Guide

Skim the passage for opinion words. Underline them. How many do you find?

Which statement in paragraph 1 is a fact and can be verified?

What is the one opinion stated in paragraph 4?

What does the word *must* signal throughout paragraph 5?

Do the words "we know that" in paragraph 6 indicate fact or opinion?

Circle the letter of the best answer.

1. Which of these statements from the passage is a fact?

    A. Scientific work must not be considered from the point of view of its direct usefulness.

    B. America produces many grams of radium every year.

    C. The radium is more than a hundred thousand times dearer than gold.

    D. There is always a vast field left to experimentation.

2. In paragraph 1, the statement "So it is always of interest to remember them and explain them" is an opinion because

    A. it can be verified in a reference source.

    B. it can be proven true or false.

    C. it is the viewpoint of the writer.

    D. nobody agrees with it.

3. Paragraph 4 provides

    A. only facts about radium.

    B. only opinions about radium.

    C. both facts and opinions about radium.

    D. neither facts nor opinions about radium.

4. What is the one opinion stated in paragraph 6?

    A. That particles are expelled from radium with a very great velocity.

    B. That the atoms of radium are destroyed by expulsion of these particles.

    C. That radioactive elements are constantly disintegrating.

    D. That the scientific history of radium is beautiful.

5. What two words in paragraph 7 signal opinions?

    A. *always* and *should*

    B. *field* and *experimentation*

    C. *scientific* and *work*

    D. *permanent* and *contribution*

DIRECTIONS
Read this student report on cartoon collector Art Wood. Then answer the questions on the next page.

Cartoon Collector

(1) When J. Arthur Wood, Jr. was a child, he started collecting cartoons anywhere he could find them. Sixty years later, he had 36,000 of them!

(2) Born in 1927, Wood always had a passion for cartoons. From a very young age, he practiced drawing cartoons by copying the styles of his favorite cartoonists. He even wrote to these artists and asked them to send him new cartoons. Many obliged and gave Wood their original artwork.

(3) At age 16, Wood (who is known as "Art") went to work as an elevator boy and hatrack attendant at the Library of Congress in Washington, D.C. He did this so he could have access to the library's books on cartoon and caricature.

(4) Wood was exceptionally talented and later became an award-winning editorial cartoonist himself. But he never stopped collecting other artists' works. After three decades of collecting, in 1995, he opened the National Gallery of Caricature and Cartoon Art in Washington, D.C. It was the coolest gallery in town. Unfortunately, it closed in 1997 due to insufficient funding.

(5) Wood then turned to his former employer, the Library of Congress. Today the library's Art Wood Collection of Cartoon and Caricature contains approximately 36,000 original cartoon works by more than 2,800 artists. It is the largest private collection of original cartoon art in the world. It is the most treasured jewel in the library.

(6) The cartoons in the collection are the funniest in the world. They include political cartoons, comic strips, and caricatures. There are even drawings from animated cartoons, such as Walt Disney's 1937 "Snow White and the Seven Dwarfs."

(7) Some of the pieces date back to the 1740s. Others are by contemporary cartoonists, such as Lynn Johnston, who created the "For Better or For Worse" comic strip, and Charles Shulz, creator of "Peanuts." Several Pulitzer Prize-winning cartoonists are represented as well. They are the most amazing cartoonists in the whole collection.

Circle the letter of the best answer.

1. The facts in this report

   A. express a viewpoint about Art Wood.

   B. describe the insides of the Library of Congress.

   C. give information about Art Wood and his cartoon collection.

   D. tell how the author feels about editorial cartoons.

2. The facts in this report can be verified by

   A. asking a friend about Art Wood.

   B. getting your teacher's viewpoint on Art Wood.

   C. looking up newspaper articles about Art Wood.

   D. looking for signal words.

3. What is the author's opinion about Art Wood's cartoon drawing abilities?

   A. That he was a bad cartoonist as a young boy.

   B. That he never should have become a professional cartoonist.

   C. That his cartoons are worse than the ones in his large cartoon collection.

   D. That he is a very talented cartoonist.

4. What word signals an opinion?

   A. collection

   B. funniest

   C. world

   D. cartoons

5. The statement "Some of the pieces date back to the 1740s" in paragraph 7 is a fact because

   A. everyone knows it is true.

   B. it can be checked and verified.

   C. it expresses a personal belief.

   D. this writer never lies.

6. Which of these is NOT a fact about Art Wood's collection?

   A. It is the most treasured jewel in the library.

   B. It contains approximately 36,000 original cartoon works.

   C. It contains political cartoons, comic strips, and caricatures.

   D. It contains pieces by contemporary artists.

7. On a separate sheet of paper, rewrite the last paragraph of the report, adding three more opinions.

Lesson 9 · Predictions and Generalizations

To **predict** means to guess what will happen next based on information already given.

> Alan's cat watched carefully as Alan poured milk onto his cereal. The cat loved milk. Some milk splashed out of the bowl and onto the floor.

Prediction: The cat will lap the spilled milk off the floor.

To **generalize** means to come to a broad conclusion based on specific information already given.

> Jerry visits a small southern town. People smile and say, "Hello." People hold doors open for Jerry. If he is looking at a map, people stop and give him directions.

Generalization: Everyone in the South is friendly and helpful.

Example

Read this passage about Tina. Then answer the questions.

A Day in the Life of Tina

Every morning, Tina woke up at exactly 7:15. She did all her morning activities and went downstairs. Each morning, she had orange juice and oatmeal for breakfast. She was always at the bus stop at 8:30 to catch the bus. She came home from school at 4:00 every day. She always had a snack and watched two hours of television before dinner. Every night after dinner, she went to her room and did her homework until it was time for bed.

Circle the letter of the best answer.

1. What generalization can be made about Tina?

    A. She is adventurous.

    B. She loves school.

    C. She is a creature of habit.

    D. She has brown hair.

2. What will Tina MOST LIKELY have for breakfast tomorrow?

    A. toast and apple slices

    B. oatmeal and orange juice

    C. eggs and coffee

    D. orange juice and toast

DIRECTIONS
Read this passage about the French Revolution. Use the Reading Guide for tips. The tips can help you make predictions and generalizations. Then answer the quesions on the next page.

adapted and excerpted from

A Tale of Two Cities (1859)

by Charles Dickens

(1) People said that his face was one of the most peaceful ever seen at the guillotine. (2) Many added that he looked like a prophet.

(3) One of the other victims of the same blade—a woman—had asked, not long before her time on the scaffold, to be allowed to write down her last thoughts. (4) If he had given voice to his own thoughts, they would have been these:

(5) "I see the peaceful, useful, and happy lives for which I shall lay down my own life and never see England again. (6) I see Lucie with the child who has my name. (7) I see her father, aged but otherwise healed and at peace. (8) I see the good old man, so long their friend, enriching them in ten years with all he has and passing to his reward...

(9) "It is a far, far better thing that I do, than I have ever done. (10) It is a far, far better rest that I go to than I have ever known."

Reading Guide

How do the first and last paragraphs help you make a prediction?

....

What is the old man's "reward"?

....

How do the first and last paragraphs help you make a generalization?

Circle the letter of the best answer.

1. What will MOST LIKELY happen to the prophet-like person?

   A. He will go to sleep.

   B. He will be rescued.

   C. He will be executed.

   D. He will go to England.

2. Which words in sentence 3 BEST help you make a prediction?

   A. victim, blade, scaffold

   B. same, woman, long

   C. asked, write, last

   D. one, long, before

3. What does the narrator predict will happen to the old man in ten years?

   A. He will win money.

   B. He will die.

   C. He will marry.

   D. He will travel.

4. What generalization can be made about the prophet-like person?

   A. He is ready to face his fate.

   B. He is afraid of his future.

   C. He is a hateful person.

   D. He thinks his fate is unfair.

Step 2

You have learned that to predict means to make guesses about what will happen and to generalize means to make broad conclusions. It is important to note that not all predictions or generalizations are going to be true. The reader must verify all predictions and generalizations.

The reader may predict that spilled milk will be lapped up by a waiting cat, but it is possible that a dog will run into the room and scare the cat away.

The reader may generalize that everyone in the South is friendly based on a character's interactions, but the next person that character meets may be rude.

Example

Read the following passage about Tommy. Look for ways to make predictions and generalizations.

Tommy sat at the back of the classroom. He looked over at Karen. He'd had a crush on her for two years, but had barely had the guts to talk to her.

When the teacher called on him, Tommy blushed. He didn't like to speak in class. He stammered out an answer, then looked down.

The school dance was in two weeks. Tommy wanted to ask Karen. He'd heard that the boy she kind of liked, Eddie, had asked someone else. Maybe this was Tommy's chance. When the bell rang, he tried to psych himself up. He took a deep breath and headed over to Karen's locker.

Fill in the diagrams below to show your understanding of predictions and generalizations. On the left, put a generalization in the center circle, and details that lead to the generalization in the surrounding circles. On the right, put a prediction in the center circle, and details that lead to the prediction in the surrounding circles.

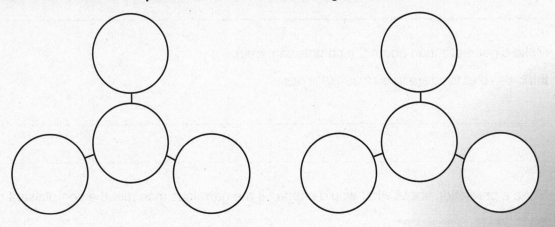

DIRECTIONS
Read this passage about characters. Then use what you have learned to make predictions and generalizations to answer the questions. Make a graphic organizer on a separate sheet of paper to organize your thoughts.

adapted and excerpted from

The Characters (circa 300 B.C.E)

by Theophrastus

III. The Garrulous Man

The Garrulous Man sits down beside someone he doesn't know and begins to praise his own wife. He continues by describing a dream he had, then tells what he had for dinner. Next, he remarks how much better people used to be, how much wheat costs, and how crowded the cities are getting. He observes that it has been good sailing weather and that more rain would be good for the crops. If you let him, he will never stop.

V. The Complaisant Man

The Complaisant Man greets you from way off, shows you more than the necessary respect, shakes your hand, and won't let go. After walking with you a little way and asking when he will see you again, he finally leaves with some words of praise. If he is called into court as a witness, he wants to please not only the person he is there to support, but also that person's opponent. This way he will seem to be impartial.

1. Make a generalization about the garrulous man.

   HINT: Look at this character's behavior.

   _____

   _____

2. Make a generalization about the complaisant man.

   HINT: How does this character act toward other people?

   _____

   _____

3. Make a prediction about what would happen if the garrulous man met the complaisant man.

   HINT: Use your generalizations.

   _____

   _____

Step 3

DIRECTIONS
Read this passage about a Greek myth. Then answer the questions.

Cassandra

According to Greek mythology, the god Apollo fell in love with a woman named Cassandra. To win her over, he gave her the gift of knowing the future. She accepted his gift but did not return his love, so Apollo cursed her so that no one would believe what she said.

When the city of Troy was attacked, Cassandra foresaw its downfall. No one believed her. Then in the middle of the night, the attackers entered the city and destroyed it.

After the Trojan War, Cassandra returned to Athens with a king named Agamemnon. She warned him repeatedly that something terrible would happen to him there, but, of course, he did not listen.

Circle the letter of the best answer.

1. What generalization can be made about Apollo?

   A. He is spiteful.

   B. He is kind.

   C. He is funny.

   D. He is old.

2. What generalization can be made about Cassandra?

   A. She is happy.

   B. She is tall.

   C. She is unattractive.

   D. She is frustrated.

3. What will MOST LIKELY happen to Agamemnon?

   A. He will live a long time.

   B. He will die in Athens.

   C. He will become very rich.

   D. He will have a big feast.

4. What prediction can be made about Cassandra?

   A. People will finally listen to her.

   B. She will become a queen.

   C. No one will ever listen to her.

   D. She will save Athens.

DIRECTIONS
Read the passage. Use the Reading Guide for tips that can help you make predictions and generalization. Then answer the questions on the next page.

adapted and excerpted from

Bartleby, the Scrivener (1853)

by Herman Melville

I called out to Bartleby, quickly stating what it was I wanted him to do—namely to proofread a small paper with me. Imagine my surprise, no, my alarm, when without moving from his privacy, Bartleby, in an especially mild, firm voice, replied, "I would prefer not to."

I sat for a while in perfect silence, regaining my stunned senses. Immediately it occurred to me that my ears had deceived me, or Bartleby had entirely misunderstood my meaning. I repeated my request in the clearest tone I could take on. However, in quite as clear a one came the previous reply, "I would prefer not to."

"Prefer not to," I echoed, rising in high excitement and crossing the room with one stride. "What do you mean? Are you moon-struck? I want you to help me compare this sheet here—take it," and I thrust it towards him.

"I would prefer not to," he said.

I looked at him steadily. His face was thin, and his gray eye was dimly calm. Not a wrinkle of distress rippled him. If there had been the least uneasiness, anger, impatience or disrespect in his manner; in other words, if there had been anything ordinarily human about him, I would have violently dismissed him from the office. However, as it was, I would have as soon thought of throwing my statue of Cicero outside. I stood gazing at him for a while, as he went on with his own writing, and then reseated myself at my desk. This is very strange, I thought. What should I do?

Reading Guide

What is the narrator's relationship to Bartleby?

....

What is unusual about Bartleby's behavior?

....

Based on the third paragraph, what prediction can you make?

....

Why does the narrator let Bartleby stay?

....

Is it likely that Bartleby will do what the narrator asks?

Now read each question. Circle the letter of the best answer.

1. What generalization can be made about the narrator based on the first paragraph?

   A. He has sense of humor.

   B. He likes danger.

   C. He is Bartleby's boss.

   D. He does not have a job.

2. What generalization can be made about Bartleby?

   A. He is a prankster.

   B. He is defiant.

   C. He loves his job.

   D. He is happy.

3. What generalization can be made about the narrator based on the third paragraph?

   A. Bartleby's behavior upsets him.

   B. He wears fancy clothes.

   C. He is very polite.

   D. Bartleby brings him great joy.

4. What generalization can be made about the narrator based on the last paragraph?

   A. He is cruel.

   B. He is smart.

   C. He gives Bartleby the benefit of the doubt.

   D. He is happy with how Bartleby does his job.

5. What will the narrator MOST LIKELY do?

   A. He will give Bartleby a raise.

   B. He will hire Bartleby's brother.

   C. He will quit his job.

   D. He will fire Bartleby.

DIRECTIONS
Read this passage. Then answer the questions on the next page.

Animal Friends

by Sally Gershon

Since she was a small child, Erin hated to see animals suffer. Her family always had pets, and Erin doted on them all tenderly. Animals seemed to sense her kindness. Even strays on the street would often come right up to her as if they knew her. Erin was always glad to see every one of them.

When Erin was in elementary school, she started a club for animal lovers. The members met every week. They would talk about their own pets and then walk around the town, helping strays if they could. In high school, Erin volunteered her time after school and on the weekends at local animal shelters. She took care of the animals there and tried to get people to adopt them. At the end of high school, she planned to get a job helping animals.

During college, Erin studied two hours every night. She studied more if she knew there was going to be a test. She made the Dean's List every semester. At the end of four years, Erin graduated with honors.

While she was at college, Erin adopted a dog and a cat. One day, she went down to the animal shelter and rescued them. Both animals were very happy with Erin.

After college, Erin moved to a small town. One afternoon, as she walked down the street, she saw a dog limping along the side of the road. Erin approached it. The dog was clearly injured. Erin thought it had been hit by a car. She coaxed it into the back of her own car.

Circle the letter of the best answer.

1. What generalization can be made about Erin based on the first paragraph?

    A.   Erin is a caring person.

    B.   Erin is a mean person.

    C.   Erin has brown hair.

    D.   Erin likes to play chess.

2. What generalization can be made about Erin based on the second paragraph?

    A.   Erin is a loner.

    B.   Erin does not talk to others.

    C.   Erin can organize others.

    D.   Erin is very selfish.

3. What prediction can be made based on the second paragraph?

    A.   Erin will be a secretary.

    B.   Erin will be a teacher.

    C.   Erin will open a restaurant.

    D.   Erin will be a veterinarian.

4. What generalization can be made about Erin based on the third paragraph?

    A.   Erin was a bad student.

    B.   Erin was a dedicated student.

    C.   Erin read a lot of books.

    D.   Erin had a lot of friends at college.

5. What generalization can be made about Erin based on the fourth paragraph?

    A.   Erin ignored her pets.

    B.   Erin took good care of her pets.

    C.   Erin never fed her pets.

    D.   Erin wanted to sell her pets.

6. What generalization can be made about the injured dog based on Erin's past?

    A.   The dog trusted Erin.

    B.   The dog ran from Erin.

    C.   The dog tried to bite Erin.

    D.   The dog had brown fur.

7. What MOST LIKELY happened at the end of the story?

    A.   Erin was mean to the dog.

    B.   Erin left the dog in the car.

    C.   Erin took the dog to a hospital.

    D.   Erin forgot about the dog.

8. On a separate sheet of paper, invent some details that would lead the reader to predict that Erin adopted the injured dog.

Lesson 10 • Inferences and Conclusions

An **inference** is a determination a reader makes based on the information and evidence provided in a passage. Inferences are not directly stated in a passage. They are the readers' own ideas and interpretations based on clues and evidence that are directly stated.

Example

Read this passage. Then answer the questions.

> Was it the smoked salmon? It did taste a little slimy.
>
> The low-fat cream cheese? Is cream cheese really supposed to be that chunky?
>
> A bad bagel, perhaps? Fuzzy purple spots are usually a dead giveaway.
>
> All Helga knew was that she was doubled over in the fetal position. She was clutching her stomach and letting out a soft, low moan. She needed something to ease the nausea.
>
> "Ma!" Helga shouted. "Please come here!"

Circle the letter of the best answer.

1. What can you infer about Helga?

    A. She does not like salmon.

    B. She loves cream cheese.

    C. She was doubled over in the fetal position.

    D. She has food poisoning.

2. What clue BEST supports the inference from question 1?

    A. Please come here!

    B. She needed something to ease the nausea.

    C. Was it the smoked salmon?

    D. The low-fat cream cheese?

DIRECTIONS
Read this passage about Sojourner Truth. Use the Reading Guide to help you make inferences. Then answer the questions on the next page.

Ain't I a Woman?

The Life of Sojourner Truth

The woman who renamed herself Sojourner Truth challenged injustice on a near-daily basis. Born into slavery as Isabella Baumfree in Ulster County, New York, in 1797, Truth escaped to Canada in 1827. She later returned to New York to live, and worked as a domestic servant. In her later life, she became known as an abolitionist speaker and a champion of women's rights. Following a spiritual revelation in 1843, she changed her name to Sojourner Truth.

In 1851, at a women's convention in Akron, Ohio, Truth delivered a speech entitled "Ain't I a Woman?" in which she declared, "That man over there says that women need to be helped into carriages, and lifted over ditches, and to have the best place everywhere. Nobody ever helps me into carriages, or over mudpuddles, or gives me any best place! And ain't I a woman? Look at me! Look at my arm! I have ploughed and planted, and gathered into barns, and no man could head me! And ain't I a woman?"

Women of all races and generations identified with Truth's perspective. More than 100 years after the speech, in 1981, educator and social critic Bell Hooks authored a book titled *Ain't I a Woman? Black Women and Feminism,* in which she uses Truth's speech as a starting point for a discussion of racism and sexism in modern culture.

Reading Guide

What can you guess about Sojourner Truth that is not directly stated?

How would you have dealt with Sojourner Truth's challenges?

Why would women agree with Truth's perspective?

Circle the letter of the best answer.

1. Why would Bell Hooks have written a book about Sojourner Truth?

   A. She wanted to make money.

   B. She is a feminist.

   C. She is an activist.

   D. She felt Truth's story was worth retelling.

2. Why would Truth have asked "Ain't I a woman?"

   A. to point out unfair economics

   B. to point out sexism

   C. to point out racism

   D. to point out sexism and racism

3. Why would Sojourner Truth have returned to New York?

   A. She was recaptured and sent back.

   B. New York outlawed slavery.

   C. She wanted to return to her owner.

   D. She did not like Canada.

4. Based on the passage, you can infer that Truth's work

   A. benefited many people.

   B. was mostly ignored.

   C. got her into trouble with the government.

   D. made her wealthy.

Readers make inferences based on information and evidence provided in a passage. A **conclusion** is an overall opinion or decision about what is happening in a passage. Conclusions can be built upon one or more inferences.

Example

DIRECTIONS
Read the following passage. Look for details that can help you draw conclusions.

Mario and Kasey

Mario walked out of the house with a spring in his step and his puppy, Kasey, firmly secured to a crimson leash. It was early in the morning, time for Kasey's inaugural walk at the park. Mario hadn't managed to step off the front porch when he became entangled in Kasey's leash, and then the dog half-pulled him down the steps, where he fell onto his hands and knees, right into a puddle. Now, the knees of his pants were wet, and the cool morning air was giving him a chill he could feel deep in his bones.

Mario held Kasey's leash steadfastly in his left hand, as the enthusiastic dog dragged him along the path that wound in the direction of the dog run. The park was full of puddles and mud, as it had been pouring all week, leaving Mario to think it possible that he might never feel dry again. Immediately after they reached the dog run, Kasey saw another dog and tore away from Mario, trailing his leash behind him.

At least they were inside the dog run, thought Mario, with exasperation. He looked around and saw Jenny, who had brought her bulldog, Warren, to the park. Warren seemed to exhaust himself standing up. He never actually ran at the dog run, but he enjoyed visiting with the other dogs, and sat at Jenny's feet waiting for his friends to appear before him. Momentarily, Kasey came bounding up to them, wagging his tail at Jenny and Warren. Kasey was hardly recognizable, as he was covered in mud from head to tail.

Fill in the boxes below with one inference for each paragraph and a single conclusion about the passage as a whole.

Paragraph 1	
Paragraph 2	
Paragraph 3	
Overall Conclusion	

DIRECTIONS
Read this passage about bioremediation. Use what you have learned about inferences and conclusions to answer the questions. Make a graphic organizer on a separate sheet of paper to organize your thoughts.

Bioremediation: The Natural Cleanup Method

Environmental pollution is a growing problem in many parts of the world today. Many of the processes used in agriculture and industry release pollutants into the environment. Some pollutants are harmful only in large amounts, while others, such as chemical dioxins, are dangerous to humans even in smaller amounts. Dioxins are called "persistent chemicals," because they break down very slowly, if at all. This makes their presence more dangerous to humans. They are often produced during the burning of substances that contain chlorine. This can include most burning fuels, such as wood, coal, and gas.

What can be done to remedy such pollution? Biological remediation (bioremediation) is a safe and effective way of dealing with dioxins. This method uses the natural processes of microbes and plants to clean up ground water, tainted soils, sludge, and industrial waste. Scientists have found that certain microbes break down pollutants and make them less harmful. This method was used with great success in Hanahan, South Carolina, after a 1975 leak from a military storage space. About 80,000 gallons of jet fuel seeped into underground water sources. Using bioremediation, this toxic threat was reduced by 75 percent.

1. What types of problems might environmental pollution cause?

    HINT: Pollution affects all living things.

    _____

    _____

2. What industries are the most likely polluters?

    HINT: Most of the pollutants are chemicals.

    _____

    _____

3. What might happen if nothing is done to control pollution?

    HINT: Use details from the story and what you know to make a reasonable inference.

    _____

    _____

Step 3

DIRECTIONS
Read this passage. Then answer the questions.

Alice in the Hallway

adapted from an excerpt from *Alice's Adventures in Wonderland* (1865) by Lewis Carroll

Fortunately, Alice was uninjured, and she quickly regained her footing. She glanced upward, but only darkness loomed overhead. There wasn't a moment to lose, so Alice sped away like the wind, just in time to hear the creature mutter, "Oh my ears and whiskers, how late it's getting!" She was close behind when she turned the corner, but the rabbit disappeared. She found herself in an elongated, low hall, which was lit up by a row of lamps.

Poor bewildered Alice was utterly amazed to find herself surrounded by numerous doors in the hallway, all of which were unfortunately locked. After journeying from end to end, checking each, she trod sadly down the middle, wondering how she was ever to get out again.

Suddenly, she happened upon a curious three-legged table, constructed entirely of solid glass; there was nothing atop it except a miniature golden key, and Alice's first thought was that it might belong to one of the doors; but, alas! Either the locks were oversized, or the key was undersized, but regardless, it wouldn't open any of them. However, on the second time around, she came upon an unusually small door, approximately fifteen inches high. She tried the little golden key in the lock, and to her great delight it fit!

Circle the letter of the best answer.

1. What can you infer happened to Alice just before the passage begins?

   A. She was eating.

   B. She fell.

   C. She was playing.

   D. She got sick.

2. Reread the second paragraph. Alice MOST LIKELY felt

   A. sore.

   B. hungry.

   C. trapped.

   D. sleepy.

3. The rabbit Alice was chasing in the first paragraph MOST LIKELY

   A. escaped into the small door.

   B. did not know Alice was chasing him.

   C. was running late.

   D. was ahead of schedule.

4. You can conclude that this story was written for

   A. senior citizens.

   B. scientists.

   C. teachers.

   D. children.

DIRECTIONS
Read the passage. Use the Reading Guide for tips that can help you draw inferences and conclusions. Then answer the questions on the next page.

Do the Twist!

The Story of Chubby Checker

Ernest Evans was born in Spring Gulley, South Carolina, and later the family moved to South Philadelphia, Pennsylvania. One day, his mother brought him to see Sugar Child Robinson, a young boy who played the piano. Evans decided to become a musician, too, and at the tender age of 11, he started a harmony group that sang together on the street corner. Later, his boss at one of his after-school jobs gave him the nickname "Chubby."

Soon after, a popular music host named Dick Clark asked Chubby to make a private recording to send out as a holiday greeting. The record was well-received, and Chubby got a recording deal. Dick Clark's wife thought that "Chubby Evans" wasn't a very catchy name. She suggested he change it to Chubby Checker (a play on the name of another famous recording star, Fats Domino). Chubby Checker went on to record a song called "The Twist." The producers didn't think it would do well, but Checker worked hard to promote it, and a year later it was a number one hit.

"The Twist," both the song and the dance, became a national phenomenon. Soon, other performers were copying the idea. Dozens of "twist" songs were recorded, and Checker himself did several variations, including "Let's Twist Again."

Reading Guide

When you read this paragraph, ask yourself what influenced Evans's interest in music.

When making inferences, think about what you would be doing or feeling if you were Evans.

If you understand what is happening, but the story does not specifically say it, you are making an inference or conclusion.

Circle the letter of the best answer.

1. Based on the story, you can conclude that Chubby Checker

    A. wishes he never recorded "The Twist."

    B. is the most popular recording star of all time.

    C. tries hard in everything he does.

    D. is a fun guy who likes people.

2. Based on the story, you can infer that young Ernest Evans

    A. dreamed of playing the saxophone.

    B. was pressured to perform by his family.

    C. wished the family never moved to South Philadelphia.

    D. was impressed and inspired by Sugar Child Robinson.

3. Using information from the story, explain why Chubby Checker and other performers MOST LIKELY recorded a variation of "The Twist" after it became a hit.

_____

_____

_____

_____

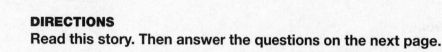

DIRECTIONS
Read this story. Then answer the questions on the next page.

Lobster Dinner

Mara and her dog, Clementine, came through the door. Mara released Clementine from the leash, and the animal scampered down the hallway. Suddenly, Mara heard her mother shrieking. Rushing in, Mara discovered her mother down on all fours, reaching beneath the table toward an angry-looking lobster. Clementine scurried in to investigate, spied the lobster, and then immediately began barking ferociously. A second lobster was scuttling across the countertop, away from the boiling pot of water on the stovetop.

"Ouch!" yelled Mara's mom.

Mara hurried to the cupboard and hauled out an enormous stainless steel stockpot. She placed it on the floor, and then leapt toward the counter, where the other lobster was still attempting its escape. Mara removed two sturdy wooden spoons from a drawer and tossed one to her mother.

With her own spoon, Mara poked and pushed the countertop lobster, encouraging him slowly toward the sink. Finally, he reached the edge, and toppled into the pot dramatically. Then, Mara joined her mother on the floor. The lobster had retreated to a corner and was clamping the opposite end of the wooden spoon Mara's mother was still firmly grasping. Mara began prodding and pushing the lobster toward the stockpot. He kept a firm grip on the wooden spoon, but slowly began backing up in the direction of the stockpot, until finally, his tail and part of his body were inside. Mara quickly tipped the stockpot upright, and the lobster slid completely inside, still holding the wooden spoon.

Mara picked up the pot gingerly, and placed it on the countertop. Clementine just kept barking in the excitement.

"Mom, what were you thinking?" asked Mara, sighing.

"I wanted to cook lobster for dinner, couldn't you tell?" she asked, with a grin.

Circle the letter of the best answer.

1. Mara's mom has probably

    A. cooked lobster many times before.

    B. cooked only seafood in her lifetime.

    C. never cooked lobster before.

    D. gotten pinched by many lobsters.

2. Where had Mara MOST LIKELY been before the start of the first paragraph?

    A. at the grocery store

    B. returning her fishing pole to the dock

    C. eating a crab cake sandwich

    D. taking Clementine for a walk

3. What can you conclude about Mara?

    A. She helps her mom out often.

    B. She does not like walking Clementine.

    C. Lobster is her favorite food.

    D. She will never eat lobster again.

4. The story probably takes place

    A. on a dock.

    B. in a kitchen.

    C. in a bathroom.

    D. at a beach.

5. If Mara had not come home when she did,

    A. the lobsters would not have escaped.

    B. Clementine would have eaten the lobsters.

    C. Mara's mom would have had a harder time catching the lobsters.

    D. she would have been grounded.

6. What can you conclude about Mara's mom?

    A. She loves her daughter.

    B. She loves Clementine.

    C. She is a master chef.

    D. She struggles in the kitchen.

7. Why did Mara's mom yell "Ouch!"?

    A. Her knees hurt from crawling on the floor.

    B. The lobster pinched her.

    C. Clementine bit her.

    D. She got hit by the wooden spoon Mara threw to her.

8. You could infer that

    A. Clementine will eat all the lobster.

    B. Mara and her mom will cook the lobsters together.

    C. the lobsters will all escape again.

    D. Mara and her mother will put on some records and dance.

Lesson 11 • Summarize and Paraphrase

A **summary** is a short retelling of a passage. It includes the main idea and most important details. A writer must paraphrase when writing a summary. A **paraphrase** is a restatement in the reader's own words to avoid plagiarizing.

Example

Read this passage about a radio drama. Then answer the questions.

War of the Worlds

The War of the Worlds was a novel written by H.G. Wells about a Martian invasion on Earth. It was adapted as an on-air radio drama and performed as a Halloween special in 1938. The radio drama retold Wells's story of a Martian invasion on Earth. The drama was presented as news bulletins that interrupted the CBS radio station's standard music programming. It was meant to be entertainment, but many people believed the news bulletins were real and aliens were actually attacking. It is believed that the radio show caused mass hysteria in the United States.

There is debate about the degree of hysteria the radio show created. Some say people were panicking in the streets. Others say the program caused major social disturbances in the areas around New York and New Jersey where the drama was set. Many listeners didn't hear or comprehend the opening credits and disclaimer that said the news bulletins were meant as dramatic entertainment. It is also said that tension at a time close to America's involvement in World War II contributed to the hysteria.

Circle the letter of the best answer.

1. What is the BEST summary for the passage?

   A. H.G. Wells wrote *The War of the Worlds.*

   B. It is believed that *The War of the Worlds* caused mass hysteria in the United States.

   C. People are afraid of an alien attack.

   D. News bulletins should not be used as dramatic entertainment.

2. Write a summary of the second paragraph. Paraphrase the sentences and write the summary in your own words.

   _____

   _____

   _____

   _____

DIRECTIONS
Read this passage about mondegreens. Use the Reading Guide to help you pick out features of a summary. Then answer the questions on the next page.

Misheard Lyrics

You probably know what a mondegreen is even if you are not familiar with this term. A mondegreen is a word or phrase that has been misheard or misinterpreted in a song lyric. The new lyric or phrase has a different meaning that is often comical.

For example, the song "Rudolph, the Red-Nosed Reindeer" has a lyric that goes "all of the other reindeer, used to laugh and call him names." Many bemused parents have reported hearing their children sing it as "Olive, the other reindeer, used to laugh and call him names."

The word *mondegreen* is a mondegreen. It comes from a misheard lyric from the old song "The Bonnie Earl O'Murray." Sylvia Wright, a columnist, wrote in 1956 that she had been singing a lyric wrong since childhood. Instead of "They had slain the Earl O'Murray, and laid him on the green," she sang "They had slain the Earl O'Murray, and Lady Mondegreen." Since then, these misinterpretations have been called mondegreens.

Some people think that the first line of our national anthem is "Jose, can you see?" Others believe that the line "O'er the ramparts we watched" is supposed to be "Oh, the red parts we washed." Silly, isn't it?

Reading Guide

Is the main idea of the article explained in the first paragraph?

....

Would the origin of the word *mondegreens* be an important detail to mention in a summary?

....

Should you include every example of a mondegreen in a summary?

Circle the letter of the best answer.

1. Which sentence BEST summarizes the third paragraph of this article?

    A. "The Bonnie Earl O'Murray" is an old song.

    B. The word *mondegreen* was coined in 1956.

    C. Sylvia Wright thought that "laid him on the green" was "Lady Mondegreen."

    D. The word *mondegreen* comes from a misunderstood lyric of an old song.

2. Read this sentence from the article.

    "The new lyric or phrase has a different meaning that is often comical."

    Which sentence BEST paraphrases this sentence.

    A. The new lyric is different.

    B. The new lyric's meaning is different and funny.

    C. The new lyric is misheard.

    D. The new lyric is often comical and has a different meaning.

3. Write a summary of the article. Be sure to paraphrase the author's original wording.

    _____

    _____

    _____

    _____

A good summary gives readers enough information to understand what the original passage was about without reading it. Never copy a sentence directly from the original passage. This may be considered **plagiarism**—claiming someone else's work as your own, which is a crime. Use your own words to avoid the possibility of plagiarizing.

Example

Read the following article about rogue waves. Look for information to include in a summary.

Rogue Waves

Rogue waves are gigantic ocean waves that come out of nowhere and can reach nearly 100 feet tall, which is about the height of a 10-story building.

Rogue waves were considered to be a thing of legend until New Year's Day in 1995, when one was witnessed and measured at the Draupner oil platform off the coast of Norway, in the North Sea. The rogue wave caused some minor damage to the oil platform. Based on its size and strength, it was considered by experts to be a 1 in 200,000 wave.

Rogue waves are a threat even to all ships and even large ocean liners. With a maximum height of 100 feet or more and a trough that seems to stretch to the bottom of the ocean, these waves are capable of capsizing and sinking large ships in the blink of an eye.

DIRECTIONS

Fill in the boxes below with a one-sentence summary of each paragraph from the article. Be sure to paraphrase the article and use your own words.

Paragraph 1	
Paragraph 2	
Paragraph 3	

DIRECTIONS
Read this passage about cryptozoology. Use what you have learned about summarizing and paraphrasing to answer the questions. Make a graphic organizer on a separate sheet of paper to organize your thoughts.

Cryptozoology

Cryptozoologists search for and investigate the possible existence of cryptids, which are animals that have never had their existence verified by scientific observation. Cryptozoologists also search for animals that are believed to be extinct.

Bernard Heuvelmans is one of the first widely-known cryptozoologists. He believed the study should be pursued by science with an unbiased, interdisciplinary approach. Heuvelmans felt urban folktales about monsters and unexplained beasts could be used as a basis for research. Urban legends are often surrounded by exaggeration and outright lies, but they are sometimes created with an aspect of truth that offers some potential for scientists to study elusive cryptids.

The Loch Ness Monster, Bigfoot, and Chupacabra are examples of widely-reported cryptids. Many people identify the Loch Ness Monster as a plesiosaur, a long-necked aquatic dinosaur believed to have gone extinct 65.5 million years ago. Bigfoot is believed to be a 7-to-10-foot tall primate inhabiting the Pacific Northwest United States and southwestern Canada. Chupacabra is a fairly new cryptid that is said to drink the blood of its prey. Descriptions vary widely—it has been described as a dog, humanoid, and reptile and has allegedly been seen in Latin America, Mexico, and the United States.

1. Paraphrase the first sentence of the article.

    HINT: Restate the main idea of the sentence in your own words.

    _____

    _____

2. Summarize the scond paragraph.

    HINT: A summary includes the main idea and only the most important details.

    _____

    _____

3. Summarize the last paragraph.

    HINT: Do not include specific, minor details.

    _____

Step 3

DIRECTIONS

Read this section of F. Scott Fitzgerald's *This Side of Paradise* (1920). Then answer the questions.

excerpted from

This Side of Paradise

by F. Scott Fitzgerald

⓵ The street numbers of Riverside Drive were obscured by the mist and dripping trees from anything but the swiftest scrutiny, but Amory had finally caught sight of one— One Hundred and Twenty-seventh Street. ⓶ He got off and with no distinct destination followed a winding, descending sidewalk and came out facing the river, in particular a long pier and a partitioned litter of shipyards for miniature craft: small launches, canoes, rowboats, and catboats.

⓷ He turned northward and followed the shore, jumped a small wire fence and found himself in a great disorderly yard adjoining a dock. ⓸ The hulls of many boats in various stages of repair were around him; he smelled sawdust and paint and the scarcely distinguishable fiat odor of the Hudson. ⓹ A man approached through the heavy gloom.

Circle the letter of the best answer.

1. How is sentence 1 BEST paraphrased?

   A. Riverside Drive was obscured.

   B. Amory saw mist and dripping trees.

   C. Amory saw One Hundred and Twenty-seventh Street despite the obscuring mist.

   D. One Hundred and Twenty-seventh Street was misty.

2. What is the BEST summary of sentence 2?

   A. Amory walked down to the river and up to a pier.

   B. Amory saw several boats.

   C. A winding sidewalk led down to the river.

   D. Amory had no distinct destination.

3. How is the second paragraph BEST summarized?

   A. Amory found himself in a boatyard adjoining a dock, and a man approached.

   B. The man did not make Amory leave the yacht club.

   C. Amory did not know where he was.

   D. A man approached Amory.

DIRECTIONS
Read the passage. Use the Reading Guide for tips that can help you summarize and paraphrase the text. Then answer the questions on the next page.

Harrisburg, PA

The capital of Pennsylvania is Harrisburg, a city perched on the Susquehanna River. Harrisburg was founded in 1710 by John Harris, and today has a population of more than 50,000 people. Harris's son-in-law, John Maclay, created the layout for the city in 1785.

Harrisburg has played an important role in several American historical events, including the Industrial Revolution and the Civil War. The capitol building was destroyed by fire in 1897. The current capitol complex was opened in 1906 and includes a four-acre park. The hall of the House of Representatives was painted with five murals by Edwin Austin Abbey. These murals feature many of the state's most famous citizens.

Modern Harrisburg has many attractions. The city's urban center is Market Square, the site of stores and public gardens. The State Museum of Pennsylvania, the Whitaker Center for Science and the Arts, and the National Civil War Museum are also located in Harrisburg, and attract many visitors to the city. The National Civil War Museum is the largest museum with a Civil War focus in the world, and attracts visitors from all over the country. The *Pride of the Susquehanna*, a paddlewheel boat, is another popular tourist attraction, offering guided tours along the river with a fine view of the city. The city shores of the Susquehanna comprise a five-mile-long public park. AA baseball can be found on City Island in the Susquehanna River, where the Harrisburg Senators play in Riverside stadium.

The island is accessible by bridge, and is home to 63 acres of park land, including a miniature golf course, a swimming area, a carousel, and three marinas.

Reading Guide

Which sentence in the first paragraph includes a detail you would include in your summary of this selection?

Which details would be included in a summary of the article as a whole?

Would each attraction be listed in a summary of this paragraph?

Circle the letter of the best answer.

1. Which of the following would be the MOST important detail to include in a summary of this selection?

   A. Harrisburg has played an important role in several American historical events, including the Industrial Revolution and the Civil War.

   B. The Civil War was fought in the 1860s.

   C. You can view the city from a paddlewheel boat.

   D. City Island offers baseball, swimming, and golf.

2. Which statement BEST summarizes the main idea of the first paragraph?

   A. John Harris founded Harrisburg in 1710, and today it is a city of 50,000.

   B. Harrisburg is the capital of Pennsylvania.

   C. Harrisburg, the capital of Pennsylvania, has many historical and cultural attractions.

   D. John Maclay was John Harris's son-in-law.

3. Which of the following would be the MOST important detail to include in a summary of the third paragraph?

   A. The State Museum of Pennsylvania, the Whitaker Center for Science and the Arts, and the National Civil War Museum are also located in Harrisburg, and attract many visitors to the city.

   B. The *Pride of the Susquehanna,* a paddlewheel boat, is another popular tourist attraction.

   C. The city shores of the Susquehanna comprise a five-mile-long public park.

   D. AA baseball can be found on City Island in the Susquehanna River.

4. Which statement BEST summarizes the main idea of the third paragraph?

   A. Harrisburg is accessible by bridge and ferry.

   B. Harrisburg has many historical and cultural attractions.

   C. Harrisburg has many museums.

   D. AA baseball can be found on City Island.

DIRECTIONS

Read this adapted excerpt from L. Frank Baum's *The Wonderful Wizard of Oz* (1900). Then answer the questions on the next page.

The Wizard of Oz

(1) It was very dark, and the wind howled horribly around her, but Dorothy found she was riding quite easily. (2) After the first few whirls around, and one other time when the house tipped badly, she felt as if she were being rocked gently, like a baby in a cradle.

(3) Toto did not like it. (4) He ran about the room, now here, now there, barking loudly; but Dorothy sat quite still on the floor and waited to see what would happen.

(5) Once Toto got too near the open trap door, and fell in; and at first the little girl thought she had lost him. (6) But soon she saw one of his ears sticking up through the hole, for the strong pressure of the air was keeping him up so that he could not fall. (7) She crept to the hole, caught Toto by the ear, and dragged him into the room again, afterward closing the trap door so that no more accidents could happen.

(8) Hour after hour passed away, and slowly Dorothy got over her fright; but she felt quite lonely, and the wind shrieked so loudly all about her that she nearly became deaf.

(9) At first she had wondered if she would be dashed to pieces when the house fell again; but as the hours passed and nothing terrible happened, she stopped worrying and resolved to wait calmly and see what the future would bring. (10) At last she crawled over the swaying floor to her bed, and lay down upon it; and Toto followed and lay down beside her.

(11) In spite of the swaying of the house and the wailing of the wind, Dorothy soon closed her eyes and fell fast asleep.

Circle the letter of the best answer.

1. What is the BEST summary of the first sentence?

   A. The weather was bleak and dangerous.

   B. Dorothy felt like a baby in a cradle.

   C. The wind was howling loudly.

   D. Dorothy and Toto were being blown around by the wind.

2. What is the BEST way to paraphrase sentence 4?

   A. Dorothy remained calm.

   B. Toto ran around barking.

   C. Dorothy ran around barking, but Toto remained calm.

   D. Toto ran around barking, but Dorothy remained calm.

3. What is the BEST way to summarize paragraph 3?

   A. Toto fell through the trap door, but Dorothy saved him.

   B. The high air pressure injured Toto.

   C. Toto fell through a hole in the floor.

   D. Dorothy saved Toto's life.

4. What is the BEST way to summarize the last paragraph?

   A. Dorothy could not sleep.

   B. The house was swaying in the wailing wind.

   C. Dorothy went to sleep in spite of the noisy winds.

   D. The wailing winds lured Dorothy to sleep.

5. Reread sentence 3. Which of the choices is an example of plagiarism?

   A. Toto did not like it.

   B. Toto didn't like it.

   C. Toto hated it.

   D. Toto liked it.

6. On a separate sheet of paper, paraphrase paragraph 2.

7. On a separate sheet of paper, write a summary of the passage. Be sure to use your own words.

Lesson 12 • Reference Materials

A **reference** is a source of information.

A **dictionary** is an alphabetical listing of words with their meanings, pronunciations, and origins.

A **thesaurus** is an alphabetical listing of words with their synonyms and antonyms.

A **periodical** is a regular publication, such as a newspaper, magazine, or journal, that gives up-to-date information about current events and topics.

An **almanac** is a book, published yearly, that contains facts about weather and events.

An **atlas** is a book of maps.

An **encyclopedia** is a collection of articles that give general information about a variety of topics.

A **Web site** is a group of related pages on the World Wide Web. This electronic resource often includes media other than text.

Example

Read this passage about a school assignment. Then answer the questions.

Belinda's Biology Paper

Belinda has to write a paper for her biology class. She has chosen cloning as her topic. She knows what it is, but not much else. She plans to go to the library this afternoon to look for some references to help her.

Circle the letter of the best answer.

1. Which reference would be MOST helpful in giving information about recent developments in cloning?

   A. dictionary

   B. thesaurus

   C. periodical

   D. atlas

2. If Belinda finds words she does not know during her research, which reference would be MOST helpful?

   A. dictionary

   B. thesaurus

   C. periodical

   D. atlas

DIRECTIONS
Read this passage about rock and roll. Use the Reading Guide to help you use reference materials. Then answer the questions on the next page.

Rock and Roll

by Josh Tiernan

(1) Rock and roll is a type of music that developed in the United States in the early 1950s. (2) It is generally a mix of country and western music and rhythm and blues music. (3) Rock and roll is most commonly played with one or two guitars, a bass, and a set of drums. (4) Other instruments, such as keyboards, are also often included.

(5) The words *rock* and *roll* both have historical origins as slang. (6) The term *rock and roll* was first used in rhythm and blues lyrics. (7) In 1951, Allen Freed, a disc jockey in Cleveland, Ohio, began using the term on the radio to describe the music.

(8) Early rock and roll recordings include "Rocket 88" by Jackie Brenston and his Delta Cats, "Rock Around the Clock" by Bill Haley and his Comets, and "Shake, Rattle and Roll" by Elvis Presley.

Reading Guide

Does this passage give general information?

Which two references give information about words?

How might you learn more about these songs?

Circle the letter of the best answer.

1. In which reference would this passage be found?

    A. encyclopedia

    B. dictionary

    C. thesaurus

    D. atlas

2. Where would you find the origins of the words *rock* and *roll*?

    A. almanac

    B. dictionary

    C. thesaurus

    D. atlas

3. Which reference could show you where Cleveland is?

    A. encyclopedia

    B. dictionary

    C. thesaurus

    D. atlas

4. Which resource might allow you to hear rock and roll music?

    A. encyclopedia

    B. Web site

    C. almanac

    D. thesaurus

Step 2

There are ways researchers can use references more quickly.

To **scan** is to look quickly through a text for specific information.

To **skim** is to look quickly through a text to get the main ideas.

Example

Read the following passage.

Tanya's European Adventure

Tanya is planning to take a trip to the Czech Republic. First she will fly to Paris, France, where her aunt lives. Then they will take a train to Prague, the capital of the Czech Republic. Tanya has never been to Europe. She wants to do some research before she goes. First, she wants to learn some general information about the Czech Republic. Next, she wants to find out what countries she and her aunt will pass through on the train. Then she wants to know what the average temperatures are in the summers there, so she will know what to pack.

Read the pieces of information in the table. Next to each, write the reference material in which it can be found.

General information	
Countries Tanya will pass through	
Average summer temperatures	

DIRECTIONS
Read this passage about the weather in New York. Use what you have learned about reference materials to answer the questions. Make a graphic organizer on a separate sheet of paper to organize your thoughts.

Field's Almanac of 1945

May 1, 1945 – New York, New York

High Temperature: 50 degrees Fahrenheit
Low Temperature: 46 degrees Fahrenheit
Average Temperature: 48 degrees Fahrenheit
Dew Point: 44.9 degrees Fahrenheit
Wind Speed: 8.4 knots
Precipitation Amount: 0 inches
Observations: Partly cloudy in the morning

1. What information related to the passage might you find in an atlas?

   HINT: The almanac entry is about a specific place.

   _____

   _____

2. What information related to the passage might you find in an encyclopedia?

   HINT: You may need general information about some of the terms.

   _____

   _____

3. What information related to the passage might you find in a dictionary?

   HINT: Are there any unfamiliar words?

   _____

   _____

DIRECTIONS
Read this passage. Then answer the questions.

Voters Undecided in Upcoming Mayoral Race

DARLINGTON – The race for mayor is coming down to the wire, as both candidates in Tuesday's election present their platforms as the answer to Darlington's problems. Polls show the townspeople are as yet undecided about whether to vote for the incumbent, Joe Cage, or his challenger, Samantha Bates.

Circle the letter of the best answer.

1. This passage is MOST LIKELY from

    A. an almanac.

    B. an encyclopedia.

    C. a newspaper.

    D. a dictionary.

2. Which reference would help you learn where Darlington is?

    A. magazine

    B. dictionary

    C. atlas

    D. almanac

3. Which reference would help the writer find another word for *candidate*?

    A. thesaurus

    B. dictionary

    C. atlas

    D. almanac

4. In which reference can you find the definition for *incumbent*?

    A. atlas

    B. dictionary

    C. almanac

    D. thesaurus

DIRECTIONS
Read the passage. Use the Reading Guide for tips that can help you use reference materials. Then answer the questions on the next page.

Take that, Einstein!

For years, physicists have believed Albert Einstein's theory that says nothing can move faster than the speed of light. Recently, though, that has been called into question.

Scientists at the NEC Research Institute in Princeton, New Jersey, claim to have exceeded the speed of light. According to Lijun Wang, in a recent experiment, a pulse of light moved through a chamber filled with gas three hundred times faster than the speed of light.

Some scientists are doubtful about the results of Wang's experiment. They say that instruments available today cannot measure such high speeds accurately. The light appears to leave the gas-filled chamber even before it enters. These scientists say that pulses of light get distorted when they pass through anything other than a vacuum.

Scientists also disagree about how useful Wang's discovery could be. If data or objects could be made to move faster than the speed of light, it would certainly have a big effect on our lives and hopes to reach distant areas of the universe. Most scientists, however, do not believe that these super-fast beams of light would be able to carry any information at all. They say it defies currently-accepted physical laws, allowing data move backward through time. Other scientists are more hopeful. They believe that this discovery could be very useful in future computer technology.

Reading Guide

Was Einstein a real person?

Does this passage give information about a recent event?

What reference might tell you the speed of light?

What resource could tell you what *vacuum* means?

What reference might tell you about these physical laws?

Circle the letter of the best answer.

1. Which reference would tell you a lot of information about Einstein?

   A. almanac

   B. atlas

   C. encyclopedia

   D. thesaurus

2. In which reference would this passage be found?

   A. scientific magazine

   B. sporting magazine

   C. scientific dictionary

   D. thesaurus

3. Which other reference might tell how fast light travels?

   A. atlas

   B. almanac

   C. thesaurus

   D. Web site

4. If the writer wanted to use a word similar to *vacuum*, she would use

   A. a thesaurus.

   B. an atlas.

   C. a magazine.

   D. a dictionary.

5. Which reference might tell you which scientists are hopeful about the experiment?

   A. thesaurus

   B. dictionary

   C. scientific Web site

   D. political Web site

DIRECTIONS
Read this passage. Then answer the questions on the next page.

Aaron stared out across the endless sand of the desert. The hot sun was just sinking below the horizon. Aaron had joined the army two years ago, but he didn't know he'd be in a place like this. It was so lonely and lifeless. Still, he would never desert. It didn't matter how unhappy he was.

desert, (DE zert) *noun* [from Latin *deserius*, solitary, waste] **1.** a dry, rainless area with very little life. **2.** an area of the ocean where no plant-life grows.; (de ZERT) *verb* [from Latin *deserere*, abandon] **3.** to leave one in trouble. **4.** to abandon a military post.

Circle the letter of the best answer.

1. An entry from which reference is shown in the passage?

    A. thesaurus

    B. dictionary

    C. encyclopedia

    D. almanac

2. Which definition applies to the author's first use of the word *desert*?

    A. definition 1

    B. definition 2

    C. definition 3

    D. definition 4

3. From which word does the noun form of *desert* originate?

    A. *deserte*

    B. *deserere*

    C. *deserius*

    D. *deserenus*

4. What lets you know the author did NOT refer to definition 2 of *desert*?

    A. There is no mention of water.

    B. There is no mention of whales.

    C. There is mention of sand.

    D. There is mention of sun.

5. Which definition applies to the author's second use of the word *desert*?

    A. definition 1

    B. definition 2

    C. definition 3

    D. definition 4

6. From what language does the word *desert* originate?

    A. Middle English

    B. French

    C. Greek

    D. Latin

7. Which reference would show you words that have similar meanings to *desert*?

    A. atlas

    B. thesaurus

    C. magazine

    D. Web site

8. On a separate sheet of paper, explain how you know the author did NOT refer to definition 3 of *desert*.

Lesson 13 • Text Features

Step 1

Text features help organize writing, add emphasis, or draw a reader's attention to key points. The chart below describes several types of text features and why they are used:

Text Features	Purpose
titles, headings, subheadings	give the main ideas of passages and parts of passages
bold, *italic*, or ALL CAPS text	emphasizes key points and key words
pictures, graphics, illustrations, charts, diagrams, tables	offer useful visual explanations of text and add entertainment value
bulleted/numbered lists	break complex ideas down into simple points

Example

Read this excerpt from a school newspaper. Then answer the questions.

Eagles Win State Championship

Freshman running back *Jason Stein* ran for 238 yards and two touchdowns as the Eagles downed the Canton Crows for the State Football Championship.

A team effort

Eagles Coach Russ Zuckerman said it took a great game from all of his players to bring the state championship home to Milning.

Score by quarters

	1	2	3	4	Final score
Eagles	0	7	3	7	**17**
Crows	0	3	0	3	**6**

Circle the letter of the best answer.

1. How many subheadings does the passage contain?

   A. none

   B. one

   C. two

   D. three

2. How many points were scored in the second quarter?

   A. 10

   B. 7

   C. 3

   D. 2

148

DIRECTIONS
Read this encyclopedia entry about The Beatles. Use the Reading Guide to help you identify text features. Then answer the questions on the next page.

The Beatles

The Beatles were a rock band from Liverpool, England. They are commonly thought of as the most successful rock band in the history of popular music[1].

Band Members

The band featured singer/songwriter/rhythm guitarist **John Lennon**, bassist/singer/songwriter **Paul McCartney**, drummer **Ringo Starr**, and lead guitarist **George Harrison**. They have sold over one billion records, cassettes, and compact discs worldwide.

Most Records Sold in America[2]

Rank	Artist	Sales
1	The Beatles	106,530,000
2	Garth Brooks	92,000,000
3	Led Zeppelin	83,620,000
4	Elvis Presley	77,280,000
5	Eagles	65,000,000

Music Career

The Beatles' career was filled with success as 40 of their songs hit number 1 on pop charts. They led the **British Invasion** of English rock bands into America and were featured on television shows like the **Ed Sullivan Show** and in feature-length movies.

[1]Source: Rolling Stone Magazine
[2]Source: http://www.classicbands.com

Reading Guide

The superscript number 1 at the end of the first paragraph indicates a footnote that is described at the bottom of the entry.

How many records did the Beatles sell in America?

How does the picture add to this encyclopedia entry?

Circle the letter of the best answer.

1. What is the title of this encyclopedia entry?

    A.   Music Career

    B.   Band Members

    C.   The Beatles

    D.   Most Records Sold in America

2. Who was the Beatles' lead guitarist?

    A.   Paul McCartney

    B.   George Harrison

    C.   John Lennon

    D.   Ringo Starr

3. Which artist sold the fourth largest amount of records in America?

    A.   The Beatles

    B.   Garth Brooks

    C.   Led Zeppelin

    D.   Elvis Presley

4. Who or what is the source of the chart about American record sales?

    A.   http://www.classicbands.com

    B.   *Rolling Stone Magazine*

    C.   The Ed Sullivan Show

    D.   John Lennon

There are several other types of text features that help organize writing. **Maps** are visual representations on paper of physical locations in the world. They are useful when talking about history or geography or when explaining how to get from one place to another.

Timelines show a series of events as they happen through history. Timelines can condense several paragraphs of information into a simple visual organizer.

Parenthetical text adds extra information within parentheses ( ).

Example

Read the following passage about Negro League legend Josh Gibson.

Josh Gibson

Josh Gibson was born on December 21, 1911, in Buena Vista, Georgia. He is known in baseball circles for his prowess as a power hitter who hit close to *800 home runs.* Gibson started his baseball career in 1930 with the **Homestead Grays**[1] of the **Negro League**[2]. African Americans were barred from playing in the Major Leagues while Gibson was alive, but he was eventually elected to the **Major League Baseball Hall of Fame**[3] in 1972 and honored in Washington, D.C. (in 2007) as one of the greatest players in the history of baseball. Gibson died on January 20, 1947, at only 35 years old.

[1] The Grays were formed in 1912 and played for 38 seasons.

[2] The Negro American League gave African Americans an opportunity to play professional baseball from 1937 to 1960, before the color barrier was broken in Major League Baseball.

[3] A museum in Cooperstown, New York, where Major League Baseball legends are enshrined.

Fill in the timeline below with key events from Josh Gibson's life and baseball career.

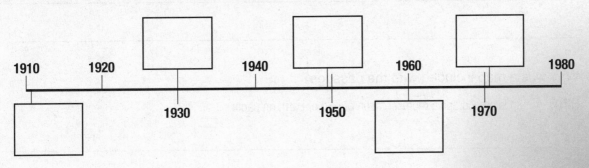

DIRECTIONS
Read this passage about the fictional island of Atlantis. Then answer the questions.

The Lost Island of Atlantis

Atlantis was a fictional[1] island in the **Atlantic Ocean.** According to legend, the island lied to the west of the **Strait of Gibraltar.** Plato's dialogues, Timaeus[2] and Critias[3] are the primary source of the legend.

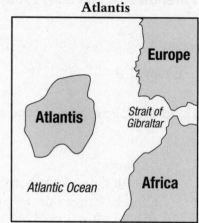

Atlantis

The Geography

The large island is said to have measured about 435 miles from end to end. It turned the surrounding area into an impassable bayou after it sunk into the sea. Before its demise, Atlantis was full of mountains to its north and along its coast.

Further Reading

The list below shows Web sites where readers can go to learn more about Atlantis.

- http://www.britannica.com/eb/article-9010107/Atlantis
- http://www.pantheon.org/articles/a/atlantis.html
- http://www.theoi.com/Phylos/Atlantes.html

[1] Most modern day scholars agree the island did not exist, but there still is some dispute over this.

[2] Plato's dialogue that offers speculation on the nature of the physical world.

[3] Plato puts forward the legend of Atlantis in this dialogue.

1. What is the most common text feature in this passage? How does it help to organize information?

   HINT: Look for words set off in special type.

   _____

   _____

2. Why was a map included with the passage?

   HINT: A map is a geographic representation of part of Earth on paper.

   _____

   _____

3. What is the purpose of the bulleted list?

   HINT: Remove the bullets and list the items in a sentence.

   _____

   _____

DIRECTIONS
Read the passage about the branches of government. Then answer the questions.

U.S. Government Branches

In the United States, the government is broken down into three branches, all of which have equal power. The branches of government are the **judicial**, the **legislative**, and the **executive**. This split provides for a separation of power so that no one person, or branch, has too much control over government, and each branch can operate independently of the other two. A system of checks and balances (also known as separation of powers[1]) exists among the three branches. This makes it possible for one branch to check the powers of the other two, limiting or amending their acts in order to maintain the balance of power.

[1] A model of government for democratic states.

Circle the letter of the best answer.

1. The words *U.S. Government Branches* are an example of

   A. a title.

   B. a subheading.

   C. a chart.

   D. an outline.

2. Why did the author bold the words *judicial, legislative,* and *executive*?

   A. The author is not sure what these words mean.

   B. The author wants students to write these words down.

   C. The author wants to highlight the importance of these words.

   D. The words are spelled wrong.

3. The expression "separation of powers" is

   A. a branch of U.S. government.

   B. a part of the executive branch.

   C. the absence of political power.

   D. a model of government for democratic states.

4. What feature does the author use to define "checks and balances"?

   A. boldface words

   B. parenthetical text

   C. timeline

   D. graph

DIRECTIONS
Read the passage. Use the Reading Guide for tips that can help you interpret text features. Then answer the questions on the next page.

Ancient Khmer Temples

In Southeast Asia, there was at one time an empire named the *Khmer Empire*. The Khmer were the rulers of the region that today includes the nation of Cambodia. They ruled the area between roughly 900 and 1200 A.D. Their primary city was called *Angkor*. The city contained many beautiful temples made of stone, which after the 1200s became deserted.

Angkor Wat

Over time, the jungle grew, and the thick forest concealed the city's fabulous architecture. This condition lasted for centuries. Only a few people were aware of the architectural treasures that lay hidden.[1] One of the greatest temples built by the Khmer was called *Angkor Wat*, which contains a large temple area and five stone towers. Angkor Wat was built during the 1100s and was an elaborate stone temple built for an important Hindu deity. Sandstone sculptures depict stories and myths of the Khmer people and the Hindu religion. The temple is recognized as one of the finest architectural masterpieces ever created.

Visiting Today

It is possible to visit Angkor Wat today: about one million tourists visit each year from all over the world. There are several organizations that lead tours, and you can find information about them on the Internet.[2]

Angkor

★ Angkor Wat

[1] A Frenchman named Henri Mahout discovered the temples in 1860 and reopened them.

[2] Today one of the most challenging issues is trying to preserve the temples. The jungle is constantly taking root in the old structures and cracking them.

Reading Guide

What is the first text feature in this article?

Identify the text features in this section.

What information can you find on the map?

Circle the letter beside the best answer.

1. Why are the terms "Khmer Empire," "Angkor," and "Angkor Wat" written in a different kind of type?

   A. to make the article more interesting

   B. to show that these are all locations

   C. to show that these are foreign words

   D. to emphasize these as key words

2. Which fact is on the map?

   A. the name of the closest river to Angkor Wat

   B. the boundaries of the original Khmer Empire

   C. the location of Angkor Wat within Angkor

   D. the location of Angkor within the Khmer Empire

3. The subheading "Visiting Today" shows the reader that

   A. the second paragraph is about a famous temple.

   B. the third paragraph is about visits to Angkor in ancient times.

   C. the city of Angkor is a wonderful place to travel.

   D. the third paragraph is about present-day tourism in Angkor.

4. Which fact is in the footnotes?

   A. The temple is among the finest buildings ever made.

   B. The jungle serves to hide and protect the temples.

   C. Henri Mahout discovered the temples in 1860.

   D. People can visit Angkor Wat today.

5. What does the second footnote give details about?

   A. the Internet

   B. Henry Mahout

   C. travel information

   D. challenges to preserve temples

DIRECTIONS
Read this passage. Then answer the questions on the next page.

Flu Prevention Tips

You know the feeling—a fever, aches, chills, headache, sore throat. It's the flu! Every year, many young people spend time sick at home because of it. According to the CDC[1], the flu is a contagious respiratory illness caused by influenza viruses. It can cause mild to severe illness, and at times can lead to death.

Every year in the United States:

- 5% to 20% of the population gets the flu;
- more than 200,000 people are hospitalized from flu complications; and,
- about 36,000 people die from flu.

Some people, such as older people, young children, and people with certain health conditions, are at high risk for serious flu complications. Nobody likes the flu. Use these tips to stay healthy this flu season.

1. Get plenty of sleep every night. Most young people need at least 8 hours of sleep.
2. Wash your hands regularly, with soap and *hot* water.
3. Take additional vitamin C in tablets or in food such as oranges or orange juice.
4. Drink plenty of water.
5. Avoid stress, which weakens your body.
6. Exercise regularly.
7. Do not eat or drink off utensils or dishes used by sick people.
8. Avoid contact with sick people.
9. Avoid touching your face.
10. Cover your mouth when you sneeze.
11. Get a flu vaccine, if your doctor advises it.

[1]Centers for Disease Control and Prevention

Circle the letter of the best answer.

1. A drawing of a girl with a thermometer would be an example of

    A. an illustration.

    B. a header.

    C. a bar graph.

    D. a photograph.

2. Why did the author include the long numbered list at the end of the passage?

    A. to give reasons why people get sick

    B. to discuss medical terms for the flu

    C. to show what the flu looks like visually

    D. to give tips on avoiding the flu

3. The heading at the top of the page tells the reader

    A. where to go for help.

    B. what to do when sick.

    C. what the passage is about.

    D. who is best-qualified to give health care.

4. What text feature is used to organize the article's statistics?

    A. a numbered list

    B. a bulleted list

    C. a chart

    D. a timeline

5. Which of the following would be the BEST addition to this passage?

    A. a photograph of several sick people in a doctor's waiting room

    B. a graph showing how many young people get sick each year

    C. an outline of an article on flu and cold prevention techniques

    D. a map to a health clinic for both car and public transportation

6. Why is the word *hot* in a different kind of type?

    A. to emphasize its importance

    B. because it is in a numbered list

    C. because the author really means cold water

    D. to make the article more interesting

7. What is the CDC?

    A. a footnote

    B. a subhead

    C. a flu vaccine

    D. Centers for Disease Control and Prevention

8. On a separate sheet of paper, describe two new text features and explain how they could be used to improve the article.

Lesson 14 • Functional Literacy

Functional literacy includes forms that need to be filled out, labels on products, sales receipts, tables, charts, and lists you need to understand for practical purposes.

Job Application Form

PLEASE PRINT CLEARLY. ANSWER ALL QUESTIONS.   Date _____

Name _____
        Last   First   Middle

Current Address _____
    Number   Street   City   State   Zip Code

Phone Number (_____) _____   Social Security Number _____ – _____ – _____

Position applying for _____

Days/hours available to work
  MONDAY _____ TUESDAY _____ WEDNESDAY _____ THURSDAY _____ FRIDAY _____
  SATURDAY _____ SUNDAY _____

EDUCATION
List the name and address of each school you have attended and the graduation dates.

_____
_____
_____

EMPLOYMENT HISTORY

JOB TITLE			
EMPLOYER'S NAME	ADDRESS	SUPERVISOR'S NAME	DATES (from—to)
JOB TITLE			
EMPLOYER'S NAME	ADDRESS	SUPERVISOR'S NAME	DATES (from—to)

Now answer these questions. Circle the letter of the best answer.

1. For what purpose would a person fill out this form?

    A. to transfer to a new school

    B. to file a complaint

    C. to obtain a job

    D. to open a bank account

2. What information does this form NOT require?

    A. your address

    B. your guardian's name

    C. your social security number

    D. the date

DIRECTIONS
Study this rebate form. Use the Reading Guide for tips about functional literacy. Then answer the questions on the next page.

Rebate Form

GET CONNECTED COMPUTER STORE

Purchase one computer printer and receive a $25 rebate!

To receive your $25 rebate:

Mail this completed form and a copy of the receipt for the printer to the following address within 60 days of your purchase:

> Happy Returns Co.
> Attn: Rebate Redemption
> 1234 Willow Lane
> Boyertown, PA 18018

Rebate forms are processed within 6–8 weeks.

Name _____

Address _____

City_____ State _____ Zip Code _____

Telephone Number _____

Printer Serial Number _____

Limit one rebate per person. Offer valid only in the USA. Void where prohibited or restricted by law.

If you do not receive your rebate after 8 weeks, please call customer service at 800.555.0000.

Reading Guide

What is a rebate?

....

Within how much time of making this purchase can someone get this rebate?

....

Where should the rebate form be mailed?

....

What should someone do if he or she does not receive the rebate after 8 weeks?

Circle the letter of the best answer.

1. A person can get a $25 rebate for purchasing what?

    A. a computer

    B. a computer printer

    C. a computer store

    D. a store receipt

2. What does one need to do in order to get the rebate?

    A. Call the phone number at the bottom of the form.

    B. Fill out the form and take it, with the receipt for the printer, back to the store.

    C. Fill out the form and mail it, with the receipt for the printer, to the address listed.

    D. Write a letter and mail it to the address listed.

3. What information is NOT required of the person filling out the form?

    A. a telephone number

    B. the printer serial number

    C. a zip code

    D. a social security number

4. How many rebates for a computer printer are allowed per person?

    A. one

    B. two

    C. three

    D. four

In everyday life, readers come across charts, lists, and tables in many forms that give different kinds of information. These might include a schedule of concert dates, a list of community events, or a telephone directory.

When reading a chart, list, or table, carefully read all headers and titles. They provide important information about what is listed below them. Remember to read charts both across and down. Think of what specific information you are looking for, and use the headers and titles to find it.

Example

Read this portion of a credit card bill.

Credit Card Statement

Previous Balance	Payments	New Activity	**New Balance**
$137.10	$137.10	$68.83	**$68.83**

Sale Date	Reference Number	Activity Since Last Statement		Amount
10/26	QF67JY9R2	T-Shirt	Philadelphia, PA	$12.00
10/28	MG2V86112	Shoes	Cherry Hill, NJ	$30.50
10/28	DRFJ45782	Books	Cherry Hill, NJ	$16.08
10/30	NKWS26771	Lunch	Media, PA	$10.25

The bar graph shows the relative prices of the items listed above. Fill in the blanks under each bar using information from the credit card statement.

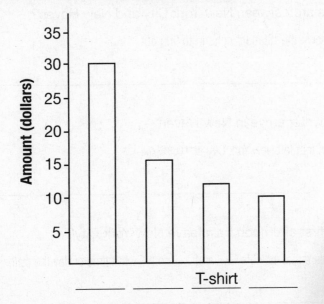

DIRECTIONS
Read this story about a train trip and study the train schedule. Use what you have learned about functional literacy to answer the questions. Make a graphic organizer on a separate sheet of paper to organize your thoughts.

All Aboard!

Last summer, when I visited my friend Marina in New Haven, Connecticut, I wasn't really sure where I was going. I was in New York City with my family on a vacation. Marina had just moved to New Haven, and she was so excited I was on the east coast. She said New Haven wasn't too far from New York City, and that I *had* to come see her!

Marina said it would be easy. I just needed to board a train in New York City on Friday morning, and she would pick me up. She told me how to find the train schedule online. It took me a while to figure it all out, but I did manage to get to New Haven, on a 10:18 AM train from New York City. Here is part of the train schedule I used:

Station	AM	AM	AM	PM	PM	PM
New York City, NY	9:18*	10:18	11:18	12:18	1:18	1:36
Stamford, CT	10:02	11:02	12:02	1:02	2:02	2:23
Darien, CT	10:10	11:10	12:10	1:10	2:10	2:29
Westport, CT	10:22	11:22	12:22	1:22	2:22	2:39
Bridgeport, CT	10:38	11:38	12:38	1:38	2:38	2:55
New Haven, CT	11:03	12:03	1:03	2:03	3:03	3:20

*Not actual train times.

1. How many stations are between New York City and New Haven?

   HINT: Read vertically down the "Station" column to find out.

2. What time did the writer arrive in New Haven?

   HINT: Look for the train that left New York City at 10:18 AM.

3. What time did the first afternoon train leave New York City?

   HINT: Look at the headers that indicate "AM" and "PM" to tell what time of day the trains leave.

Step 3

DIRECTIONS

Read this receipt from a music store. Then answer the questions.

Reading a Receipt

```
        TooCool MusicLand
        2345 E. Smith St.
          Miami, Florida


Ramblin' Sam CD                 $9.99
Ike Spike's Greatest Hits CD   $10.99
Guitar History DVD             $12.99


SUBTOTAL:                      $33.97
Sales Tax 8.375%                $2.84
TOTAL:                         $36.81
Amount tendered                $40.00
Change:                         $3.19


          July 16, 2008
    Thank you for shopping at
        TooCool MusicLand!
```

Circle the letter of the best answer.

1. How many items were purchased at TooCool MusicLand?

    A. one

    B. two

    C. three

    D. four

2. When were these items purchased?

    A. July 15, 2008

    B. July 16, 2007

    C. June 16, 2008

    D. July 16, 2008

3. How much did the Guitar History DVD cost?

    A. $10.99

    B. $12.99

    C. $33.97

    D. $36.82

4. How much money did the person making the purchases give the cashier?

    A. $40.00

    B. $33.97

    C. $36.81

    D. $3.19

DIRECTIONS
Read this menu. Use the Reading Guide for tips on analyzing functional literature. Then answer the questions on the next page.

Menu

Meat

Sirloin Steak	$12.95
Lamb Kebab	$11.95
Beef Burger	$ 7.95

Poultry

Stuffed Chicken Breast	$ 9.95
Roasted Duck	$15.95
Fried Chicken	$ 9.95

Fish

Salmon Steak	$14.95
Tuna Salad	$10.95
Grilled Swordfish	$12.95

Vegetarian

Tofu Stir Fry	$ 9.95
Bean Burrito	$ 8.95
Veggie Burger	$ 6.95

Reading Guide

How much does the beef burger cost?

Which category has the most expensive item?

How much does the tuna salad cost?

Which category has the least expensive item?

Which category has the smallest total cost?

Circle the letter of the best answer.

1. How many items are under ten dollars?

   A. three

   B. four

   C. five

   D. six

2. Which item is MOST expensive?

   A. sirloin steak

   B. roasted duck

   C. salmon steak

   D. tuna salad

3. Which category has NO items under ten dollars?

   A. meat

   B. poultry

   C. fish

   D. vegetarian

4. Which item is LEAST expensive?

   A. veggie burger

   B. beef burger

   C. tofu stir fry

   D. fried chicken

5. Which category has the GREATEST total cost?

   A. meat

   B. poultry

   C. fish

   D. vegetarian

DIRECTIONS
Read this nutrition information from the side of a cereal box. Then answer the questions on the next page.

Nutrition Facts

Serving Size: ½ cup
Servings Per Package: About 10

Amount Per Serving	Cereal	Cereal with 1 cup of skim milk
Calories	150	190
Calories from fat	45	50
% Daily Value★		
Total Fat 5g	8%	8%
Saturated Fat 1g	5%	5%
Trans Fat 0g		
Cholesterol 0mg	0%	0%
Sodium 25mg	1%	4%
Total Carbohydrate 20g	7%	9%
Dietary Fiber 3g	12%	12%
Sugars 15g		
Protein 5g		
Vitamin A	5%	10%
Vitamin C	0%	0%
Calcium	2%	15%
Iron	7%	7%
Thiamin	5%	5%
Riboflavin	8%	8%

★Percent Daily Values (DV) are based on a 2,000 calorie diet. Your daily values may be higher or lower depending on your calorie needs.

Circle the letter of the best answer.

1. What is the serving size for this cereal?

   A. one ¼ cup

   B. one ½ cup

   C. one cup

   D. ten cups

2. How many calories are in one serving of the cereal?

   A. 10

   B. 150

   C. 190

   D. 2,000

3. How much sodium is in one serving of the cereal?

   A. 1 gram

   B. 5 grams

   C. 0 milligrams

   D. 25 milligrams

4. What is the Percent Daily Value of calcium in one serving of the cereal served with one cup of skim milk?

   A. 7%

   B. 8%

   C. 10%

   D. 15%

5. What is the difference between the number of grams of dietary fiber and the number of grams of sugars in one serving of the cereal?

   A. 12 grams

   B. 10 grams

   C. 9 grams

   D. 8 grams

6. What information is NOT found in this nutrition label?

   A. the Percent Daily Value of riboflavin in one serving of the cereal

   B. the amount of calories in one serving of the cereal served with one cup of skim milk

   C. the Percent Daily Value of folic acid in one serving of the cereal

   D. the amount of calories from fat in one serving of the cereal

7. Which of these statements about the cereal is true based on the nutrition information?

   A. One serving has 5 grams of saturated fat.

   B. One serving has 2 grams of dietary fiber.

   C. There are about 10 servings per package.

   D. The cereal contains niacin.

8. On a separate sheet of paper, list three nutrition facts about this cereal. (Do not use facts already listed in these questions.)

Glossary

almanac   a book, published yearly, that contains facts about weather and events (Lesson 12)

antonym   a word that means the opposite of another word (Lesson 3)

atlas   a book of maps (Lesson 12)

author's purpose   a reason for writing (Lesson 1)

cause   a reason why something happens (Lesson 7)

chronological order   the order in which things happen over time (Lesson 5)

compare   to show how things are alike (Lesson 6)

conclusion   an overall opinion or decision about what is happening in a passage (Lesson 10)

context clue   a word or phrase near an unknown word that helps the reader understand its meaning (Lesson 3)

contrast   to show how things are different (Lesson 6)

definition   the meaning of a word (Lesson 3)

dictionary   an alphabetical listing of words with their meanings, pronunciations, and origins (Lesson 12)

effect   a result of a cause (Lesson 7)

encyclopedia   a collection of articles that give general information about a variety of topics (Lesson 12)

fact   a statement that can be proven true (Lesson 8)

figurative language   language that does not mean exactly what it says (Lesson 4)

functional literacy   includes forms that need to be filled out, labels on products, sales receipts, tables, charts, and lists you need to understand for practical purposes (Lesson 14)

generalize   to come to a broad conclusion based on specific information already given (Lesson 9)

hyperbole   an extreme exaggeration (Lesson 4)

idiom   a phrase that means something different from its literal meaning; often particular to a region or group of people (Lesson 4)

inference   a determination a reader makes based on the information and evidence provided in a passage (Lesson 10)

main idea   the most important idea in a paragraph or passage (Lesson 2)

map   a visual representation on paper of physical locations in the world (Lesson 13)

metaphor   a direct comparison that does not use *like* or *as* (Lesson 4)

opinion   a statement about someone's belief (Lesson 8)

paraphrase   a restatement in the reader's own words to avoid plagiarizing (Lesson 11)

parenthetical text   adds extra information within parentheses ( ) (Lesson 13)

periodical   a regular publication, such as a newspaper, magazine, or journal, that gives up-to-date information about current events and topics (Lesson 12)

persuasive writing   writing that tries to convince the reader to act or think a certain way (Lesson 1)

plagiarism   claiming someone else's work as your own, which is a crime (Lesson 11)

predict   to make a guess about what will happen next based on information already given (Lesson 9)

propaganda   biased, persuasive, and often dishonest writing (Lesson 1)

reference   a source of information (Lesson 12)

scan   to look quickly through a text for specific information (Lesson 12)

simile   a comparison that uses *like* or *as* (Lesson 4)

skim   to look quickly through a text to get the main ideas (Lesson 12)

summary   a short retelling of a passage that includes the main idea and most important details (Lesson 11)

supporting details   explain, describe, prove, or give examples about the main idea and topic sentence (Lesson 2)

synonym   a word which has a similar meaning to another word (Lesson 3)

text feature   a device that helps organize writing, add emphasis, or draw a reader's attention to key points (Lesson 13)

thesaurus   a reference book that provides words' synonyms and antonyms (Lesson 12)

timeline   shows a series of events as they happen through history (Lesson 13)

topic sentence   a sentence that directly states the main idea of a paragraph (Lesson 2)

Web site   a group of related pages on the World Wide Web (Lesson 12)

Notes

Notes

Notes

Notes

Notes